CW00872225

A Hundred Transgender Voices, "You are not alone."

CommUNITY
In Transition

I am greater than a sign,
More important than an emblem

Created By Best Selling Author Todd Kachinski Kottmeier
With Dr. Robyn Walters Photography By Emery C. Walters

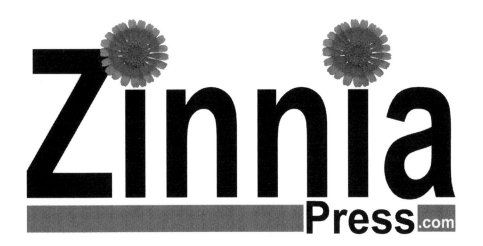

Zinnia Press
Copyright © 2014 Todd Kachinski Kottmeier

First Edition.

ISBN: 978-1-312-28916-1

Printed in the United States of America
Edited by Dr. Robyn Walters
Photography by Emery C. Walters
Intern: Casey JD Anderson
ZinniaPress.com

We chose the best, most comprehensive, insightful, or most common replies to over fifty questions. Most of the writers requested to be anonymous. To all of the contributing writers, we owe a debt of gratitude for the thousands of words donated to help inspire, motivate, and show a world, "they are not alone." For those allowing us to appreciate them by using at least a nickname, we thank:

David HOH,
Amber C.,
Ellen Shaver,
Kathy McR.,
Bekki V.,
Julie LaRoux,
Jill Micayl,
Jane S.,
Aaron Phnx,
Tori Amanda Foote,
Sifan Kahale,
Matt P.,
Cassandra Marie Frost,
Donnie C,
Kyler-Eli,
Louis M.,
Monica Harmon,
Maya Shayne,
Emery C. Walters,
Robyn Walters,
Kaylie M.,
Michelle M.,
Ashten P.,
Joanne,
Casey JD Anderson,
Hex M., and
Bryan Reed.

About Todd Kachinski

I created this book using the agenda from "CommUnity in Transition," an international transgender group created on Facebook with members seeking to save lives or offer comfort to their peers. They donated wisdom from life experience and compassion for letting others walking in their steps understand that "they are not alone." I am blessed in life, with a long proven history of helping compassionate transgender writers to share their voices. This book's content comes from the transgender community, not from me, but the community as a whole, of those willing to simply "participate" when so many transgender leaders in their community brushed them and us off under the banner of being too busy or unwilling to offer advice. New people struggling with transitioning will learn from the most incredible people who opened their hearts and minds to help strangers across the country and around the world. Many of you already know me from the hundreds of projects I do around the world. The company I founded and sold earlier this year is only a mirror, mimicking the best words shared.

About Dr. Robyn Walters

I came to this project via my husband, author Emery Walters. He is a female to male transsexual, and I am male to female. We married as one man/one woman. Within a year, we were one woman/one man. Several years later, he became seriously involved with writing, and I became the editor of his nine books and counting. That eventually led to BecHavn Publishing and our long-term relationship with its former publisher Todd Kachinski-Kottmeier. I came to my editing skills, such as they are, from a twenty-year Navy career, a U.S. Naval Academy undergraduate and MIT graduate education, and thirty-plus years as a Navy contractor. Many people helped me during my late in life transition -- mostly online in the beginning. People were there to offer advice, to lend a shoulder to cry on as my marriage fell apart, and to celebrate as I came out the other side as a proud old lady with lots of life left to live. How could I not give back? I spent some years as a transactivist, walking the halls of Congress, writing articles and letters to the editor, while supporting others contemplating or undergoing life changes. When Todd mentioned the idea for this book, I saw it as a way for many people to give back and to help others dealing with the confusion, the worry and anguish, or the pain of transition. I appreciate Todd's faith in me. He did not ask if I would like to edit the book; he just announced that I would. Now where did I put that red pen?

About Emery C. Walters

I have known I should have been - or was - really a boy since I was five years old. I buried it at puberty, locked it in a cellar deep inside myself, and felt 'him' peek or break out at rare intervals until I hit menopause, my last child left home, and I was facing the loss of a job and homelessness. Then I woke up one morning, and 'he' was here to stay, permanently. I have always written, always as a male character, and always dreamed in 'male mode'. Other than that whole "some parts not included" thing we FTM's have, I feel right for the first time.

Chapters

Each chapter represents a question created by those affected the most, the contributors of this book, to include:

1. At what age did you first question your gender?
2. When you began to question your gender identity, what was your greatest fear of speaking aloud the very first time?
3. Which person did you first approach regarding confusion of your gender identity?
4. What single term is most acceptable to define transgender or transitioning people?
5. In the beginning, which person became your best ally?
6. In the beginning, which important person in your life became your worst hater/detractor?
7. How did you handle the criticism, the anger, of the first person to express hatred?
8. In the beginning, how did you handle any anger towards less important or unimportant people in your life?
9. What is the worst thing someone did to hurt you emotionally as you transitioned?
10. What is the worst thing someone did to hurt you physically as you transitioned?
11. Top 20 Most Offensive Words
12. Describe your feelings about transgendered entertainers performing in "drag shows."
13. Can you explain a positive path to restoring family relationships lost or to maintaining family relationships during transition?
14. Who was the most important person lost during transition that later came back on their own?
15. Do your parents refer to you as your documented birth sex, or confirm your real gender?
16. If you were religious before transitioning, how did you reconcile your transitioning within formal beliefs of your

religion/church?

17. Did you lose many friends during transitioning? Explain how to stabilize emotionally your life following their loss.
18. Are you the first person in your family to transition?
19. Do you look up to anyone transitioning as a role model?
20. Before and After Photos
21. Do you believe that including transgender in the LGBT (Lesbian, Gay, Bisexual, and Transgender) acronym adds to or subtracts from the confusion?
22. How do you successfully handle discrimination during the interviewing process while looking for employment?
23. How do you successfully handle discrimination by fellow workers during employment?
24. How do you successfully handle discrimination by managers during employment?
25. How do you successfully handle discrimination by customers, clients, patrons during employment?
26. When do you tell a new friend regarding your gender correction?
27. When do you tell someone interested in dating you of your gender correction?
28. What advice do you give to someone trying to have a dating conversation?
29. Married with children (or not...).
30. How do you address the public and management when using gender assigned public restrooms and public lockers (such as a gym) that are open to everyone of the same sex?
31. How do successfully handle losing a partner unable to handle your transitioning?
32. If your partner made the transition with you but struggled later, what were the complications?
33. In the beginning, were you able to find a social network for strength?

34. Be greater than your label
35. A law in Phoenix will not apply in Chicago. A law in California will not translate to New York or Florida. Federal laws change from one day to the next. Which legal network do you use for assistance?
36. How did you pick your name, and have you corrected legal documents?
37. In the beginning, were you able to find a social network for strength?
38. What is your medicine regimen since the start of transitioning: What personal benefits, risks, and harms have you observed?
39. Do you regret transitioning?
40. Discuss positive conversations you would share with someone who is politely confused on "transgendered people."
41. What are the top books you would suggest for those transitioning?
42. Did you legally change you name to match your correct gender?
43. Have you had surgery to align your anatomy to match your correct gender?
44. If you had the operation, what were the greatest risks of the operation, regret, and recovery?
45. Many of this book's audience will be people sitting quietly in their homes, terrified to be alone, searching for an overall scope of transitioning. Many books in Chapter Forty-One will address in detail each subject on their own. "CommUnity in Transition" is you helping them by sharing your hearts and your experience. What would you say to these people to bring them comfort?

Editor's Note

More than 100 people contributed to developing and answering the questions that comprise the forty-four chapters of this book. Very few of the contributors know me personally; however, I did get to recognize several contributors by their writing styles. I hope that I did little damage to anyone's voice as I took care of grammar, spelling, and punctuation, throughout. Although I did move a word or phrase now and then, I took great care to ensure clarity without destroying the contributor's intent. Words or phrases set off by [ ] brackets are those I felt should be added to convey the intended thought. Forgive me if I mangled any of your intent and feel free to break my red pen.

Photography throughout this book by Emery C. Walters

"I dedicate thousands of hours placed in this book to

Emery and Robyn Walters.

I come from a family of many members transitioning, but the Walters held my hand as friends, to show me the remarkable people in our community struggling to become the incredible person they feel in their heart. Their spirit and determination live in this book, but thrive in their convictions.

I hope all of their wisdom in this book captures both.

Todd Kachinski Kottmeier

Chapter One

At what age did you first question your gender?

"It is important to note that sexuality is not related to gender identity. I started questioning my sexuality the same time most kids examine that subject, in puberty. But I began questioning my gender identity at around five years old. It was at that age my brother was born, showing me the differences in how he would be raised. It was also the year I entered grade school. As soon as boys and girls were separated for activities in Kindergarten, I knew I was being placed with the wrong group, although I could not explain why. Deep down I hoped one day I would go through puberty and become a man."

⚜ By age ten, I had gender confusion starting in my mind, I took a kindergarten top and forced it on to flatten the bust starting to grow. Around twelve or thirteen, I saw TV shows and tried to imagine my first kiss, only to have me turn into the boy, and the boy turn into a girl. After enough times forcing myself to think "straight girl" daydreams, I thought it was too hard and quit. So from then on, I exclusively dreamed of being a boy or man with girls or women.

⚜ I have never had to question my gender identity. I have always felt genderfluid and have always been attuned to who I am.

❧   As strange as it may sound, when growing up I never questioned it. I accepted that physically things were not right for me, but I went through life. I just lived figuring one day it would all work out. Things 50 years ago just were not discussed. I grew up with boys that treated me as a strong independent girl. I did everything I wanted. Yes, if I overheard someone speaking of "the Smith boy," I knew they were speaking of me. They were the elders of the area, and I do not think they knew what to call it.

❧   At age six. I always was curious as to why I felt uncomfortable as a boy. Girl's clothes were so much more detailed, they seemed. I felt very much like a little girl at age six. I used to raid my Mother's stuff and play dress up. The baby sitter never really checked on me; so I had periods to dress. Later in school, I found stuff when people moved out of a house. I dressed as often and as much as I could. Yes, my Father found my stuff. He beat me and threatened me with military school. It did not work, I continued to dress softer, the clothes looked prettier, and I wanted to be a fairy princess.

❧   I had known something was wrong for as long as I could remember, but my earliest memory having anything to do with gender was around six. I did not really understand it too well until I was around twelve, though.

❧   My sexuality was not questionable for me. It never entered my mind.

❧   I only began to question the relationship between gender identity and sexuality once I began to come out. That has really only been in the last ten years.

❧   Almost from as long as I can remember being aware of my gender.

❧   I never questioned it. I knew when I was four. I understood at seven. When I told my mother I was a girl, I received a speech about the expectations of the first-born male child of a generation. I spent the next forty years attempting to live up to those expectations.

❦   I questioned my gender orientation since I was a kid but put the words together "I am a GIRL" at age nine. I have always been attracted to women; so my sexual orientation has not changed.

❦   Fifty-seven, or maybe age six, depending.

❦   I became extremely interested in cross-dressing around thirteen years of age when I had enough time alone with access to female clothing and makeup. I was very aware of my interest in being only attracted to girls, and everything about them. Almost all of my friends were girls, the exception being another effeminate male friend.

❦   Ten. I was fascinated with wearing my sister's and mother's clothes and then wearing lingerie I found on clotheslines. At 15 years of age and after shaving in front of the bathroom cabinet mirror, I saw my upper body morph into that of an old woman with old saggy breasts (this came to pass).

❦   Eight or nine. I saw David Bowie on TV and was amazed. I thought that I wanted to be like him. I mean that it was him looking feminine that resonated with my sexual identity.

❦   I knew from my earliest memories - pre 5 years. However, that was in the 1950's in a small northern conservative town. I did not question my sexuality; I questioned my gender - although that is not what I knew it as at the time. However, I did know I was something other than a boy. I had explained my similarities to girls and my strangeness as a boy to having 'extra' capabilities - being able to understand both for example. As a teenager, I was always more comfortable with the girls (and vice versa). Sexuality awareness started at thirteen or fourteen I believe - I loved the girls!

❦   I started questioning my sexuality when I was younger. My mom even has pictures of me kissing people of the same sex as a kid. At the time, she thought it was normal. Once I got older and started dating, I knew that I was gay.

✿   I knew when I was about five that there was something different about me, [but it] took me a long time to figure it out.

✿   I questioned my sexuality around the time I was eleven or twelve. I am sure I would have earlier if I had had the knowledge and vocabulary to do so in the 1980's when I was growing up. In hindsight, there were several times I questioned what would grow to be my "sexuality" and with it my "gender identity."

✿   I do not remember ever questioning my sexuality. I always felt female and always liked boys. Family has told me in the past that there was no doubt that I liked boys, usually older than me. I always liked fashion, doing hair and things normally considered with girls. Growing up, my father always would say to me that one day I would make someone a good wife. It was never said as an insult, or at least, I never took it that way. Then sexuality is not something we discussed.

✿   I was around five or six if not younger.

✿   Early in elementary school I labeled myself a "tomboy" but did not really question it. My parents let me dress and play however, I wanted, with clothes and toys of both genders. In sixth grade, I had a crush on my best friend and decided I was bisexual. I continued to dress and act very masculine but did not consider the possibility that I was trans until I was a junior in high school.

✿   The only age I can truthfully post is twenty-one. I fought the desire and feelings through thirty-seven years of marriage. Most of my memory prior to that is lost except for bits and pieces restored by therapy and family members.

✿   As a little boy the age of eight, I questioned my sexuality. I never understood why I was attracted to boys. I guess my attraction came from being molested as a child. I dated girls to hide who I was because my father worked for the City of Auburndale, and my mother was a teacher at my elementary school. With my unmarried parents being so visible in our small city, I had to hide who I was at heart. Yes, I was popular as I was growing up in our small city, but never could I show my true colors. I was always told it is a sin to like the same sex. I believed them for a long time but wondered why it was a sin.

⚜   I knew I was supposed to be a boy at age five. When I hit puberty at age eleven and it did not happen, I buried my true self as deeply as I could. I decided I would play the role of a female the best I could.

⚜   I questioned my sexuality at age six. Later, after a few months on estrogen, I began to find men interesting. I ended up a non-practicing bisexual married to an FTM but interested in both males and females.

⚜   Preteen.

⚜   Really well before I was five. I remember bathing with my older sister and our differences being pointed out by our mother. At age six seeing as mine had not fallen off as hers had, I tried to take it off with a pair of scissors and a butter knife. Resulted in a trip to the ER. Not much in 1957.

⚜   I started questioning around three or four but fully decided at eighteen I could no longer live how I was. I struggled with depression and suicide. Then I found a therapist, paying out of pocket for everything.

⚜   Four years old.

⚜   I was eight years old when I first questioned my sexuality. I was one of the boys. I had my first crush on a female at this age. I was attracted to females even though I did not understand the concept since it was taboo and not to be spoken of in my household.

⚜   I first questioned my sexuality at around the age of

fourteen. I was starting to become attracted to not only boys but also girls. I held off though on the girlfriends until I was 17.

🙪   Twelve, when I learned that there was such thing as transgendered people.

🙪   I often wished I had been born male, but I do not believe I was ever confused since I did not know there was any option other than accepting what I was.

🙪   I have always known that I was different.

🙪   I started to question my sexual identity at the age of six. I knew I was different from all the other girls in school and extra activities I was in. I always felt really awkward being around them. I was one of the boys. I would hang out with the boys in my neighborhood and do guy things. I would dress like a boy except on special occasions when forced to wear a dress. I played with boy gender-based toys and wanted to take of my shirt during basketball as the other boys did. I would often look in the mirror and cry that I did not have the body to match my mentality.

Chapter Two

When you began to question your gender identity, what was your greatest fear of speaking of it aloud the very first time?

"My biggest fear was rejection. I would only ever heard the world "transgender" associated with negative images -- with freaks, sexual deviants, perverts, and serial killers in movies. I did not want my loved ones to think of me that way. As for the actual reaction, it was not nearly as bad as I expected."

❦ Fear of rejection.

❦ Growing up in rural Wyoming, I was always worried only about what my family would think.

❦ Fear of being mocked, beaten and maybe killed. This was in the mid/late 50's so there was no understanding of anything related to gender identity available. Especially not to a kid.

❦ Fear of rejection.

❦ I feel like my "sexual identity" and my "gender identity" are two separate things. My sexual identity is related to whom I am sexually attracted to, whereas my gender identity relates to the gender that I identify as. When I first began to question my "gender identity," I was honestly concerned that people would tell me that I only felt that way because I "liked the way it felt when I was a drag king," and sure enough, people did say/suggest that.

❀ I feared being around boys because of being taunted and teased. Due to the absence of body hair and my more feminine shape, boys would tease and hit on me.

❀ That I would be considered gay or a queer and that I would become an outcast. I did not really know about transgender and what that meant.

❀ I had witnessed others in school getting into big trouble because of their statements and, shall we say, "Freedom of speech" (nothing to do with gender - this was an ultra-conservative Catholic school). I wanted nothing to do with the type of retribution they suffered. I learned quickly to keep to myself, so my fear was to suffer the same fate they did.

❀ Making people that I loved worried about me or disappointed.

❀ I was terrified of the questions and looks. I did not want to end up cornered in a bathroom and beaten up because I was not the "right" gender. I heard horror stories about bullying and harassment; so I kept my mouth shut for a long time.

❀ That I would be ridiculed and humiliated by friends and family. Speaking it aloud made it real. After that, I could not live in denial of it any longer.

❀ I was not afraid to tell my best friend with whom I was doing some sexual things in play. I became afraid after that happened. In addition, I had heard homosexuality is a sin and thought my acts were similar but not the same; so I was scared anyone judge me as doing bad. My mom was phobic, thinking that all men wanted to rape her and all women. I was afraid to tell her I was not only thinking like a boy, but was doing sexual things to other kids since age six.

⚜ My greatest fear was of being physically abused, more so than I had already been by my "family" and strangers. After that was my fear of losing everything, my "friends," my "family," my "home," but most of all, my beloved animal companions.

⚜ I was NOT a sissy, as I feared many would classify me as. I saw girls playing with boy toys on occasion. Nothing was ever said to them, they were just Tom Boys having fun!

⚜ My biggest fear always has been and always will be my father's response to it. He knows now, but he is still denying it and will not say a word on the subject.

⚜ I was three when I knew I was the wrong gender. Christine Jorgensen had just returned from Denmark, and my parents and their friends all made derogatory remarks about her. I had made a connection to her and knew I could not say anything.

⚜ I am a parent of daughters; so my greatest fear was that anyone would consider that because of my gender identity I posed a risk to my children.

⚜ I did not know that I could question it; therefore, I did not talk about my feelings to anyone. I did not have a fear of speaking about it until many years later. After reading about a guy in the San Francisco Bay area who had a sex change, I decided I was going to do this, too. My greatest fear at that point was the reaction I would get telling my partner that I was male and wanted to have surgery. It turned out that I should not have worried.

⚜ My biggest fear was rejection. I had only ever heard the world "transgender" associated with negative images -- with freaks, sexual deviants, perverts, and serial killers in movies. I did not want my loved ones to think of me that way. As for the actual reaction, it was not nearly as bad as I expected. People were confused, and some were very resistant, but most were respectful. I did lose some friends along the way who expressed their disgust, but it was a small percentage in comparison to the overwhelming support I received after coming out.

✤ I did not really have a fear until I was older, and that was simply because I did not want my parents to freak out.

✤ I was not the first in my group of friends to come out as queer; so telling them I was bisexual was not hard. I was nervous telling my parents, but I would not say I was afraid. They are pretty liberal, open-minded people who had always been supportive of gay rights. My much greater fear came with coming out as trans. I was afraid of the news spreading too quickly to people I was not ready to tell yet. I was afraid my friends would use my preferred name in front of teachers or peers and that I would have to explain it in front of people (and this has indeed happened).

✤ Loss of friends and family and not knowing the why or how to act on it properly.

✤ When I turned 21-years-old and already flew the nest was the first time I spoke up about who I was. My biggest fear was my father because he was a very violent man; so to this day my father does not know. I have not seen my father since I was nine years old. When I told my mom, she said that she already knew. My mouth dropped to the floor. To the one that raised me, my Granny, I never had the heart to tell her that I was gay. See, I was the grandson of a preacher. To tell the one that raised me was too hard; my heart just would not let me tell my Granny who I really was. She was old school Southern Baptist.

✤ By the time I spoke it aloud, fifty years had passed. There was nothing to be afraid of after that much waste of life.

✤ What would my family think about me? Would they agree to my decision to live as a girl? Would they yell at me and tell me mean things? Would they disown me?

⚜ As a child, I really never questioned how I felt gender-wise; I just was. When I was teased about it, what I saw was that it just confirmed who I was. I knew who I was gender-wise; it was just others who did not see or accept it. Fear sunk in in early adulthood as the abuse of childhood became death threats rather than just physical beatings.

⚜ I was scared to lose my family; they had only ever known me as who I was not. I was scared of being killed because of narrow-minded people.

⚜ A slap on the backside from my parents.

⚜ My family not accepting me.

⚜ I was 26, married and had two kids. I finally had enough of waiting and had to say something. This happened three weeks ago, just before I turned 27. My husband said literally right back to me, "I do not care what gender you are, and I will always love you." It blew me away. I was so shocked and relieved. The world felt right.

⚜ Knowing that people like me were being locked in mental institutions for indefinite periods and left to rot (late 1950's). I was first sent to a physiatrist at seven. My folks suspected things. Remember now that they were administering electro shock at M C V hospital for people like us. I escaped only because the doctor lied for me. She told them it was a growing phase.

Chapter Three

Which person did you first approach regarding confusion of your gender identity?

"I told my best friend. She had known me for years and had watched me find myself. I knew if anyone would support me, she would. And she did. She was a little confused but made every effort to "get it" and had my back 100% of the whole time."

✜   My neighbor and friend, with whom I played sex as a pre-teen. We would be in my bed naked but for our underpants, and I would rub on her like frotting, and so I told her one day I wanted to grow up to be a man. Unfortunately, she was not a secret keeper, and in front of me told our neighbor, a man, that I wanted to be a man. He smiled and said, "Oh really?" That was last time I came out until 2012.

✜   I told my gay son about being transgendered, and he was thrilled. NOTE: that is not orientation; you are talking about identity, right?

✜   I first approached the guy I was dating. He was understanding about it, as long as I did not "try to attain a penis." If I did, our relationship was going to be over.

✜   My grandmother, I guess. For some reason she really wanted to hear about everything, including my secrets. I cannot explain why. I felt a bond; I could trust her. Yes, on occasion I would dress in her slips, have "Tea," and play dress up. She even joined in the fun, too. Also, a child psychologist at age ten and a good girlfriend I was living with when I was 19.

❧ The first person I had mentioned anything to was an ex-girlfriend of mine when I was about 24 years old. She just kind of brushed it off and never said anything about it. Now that I am out, she fully supports me and is one of my best friends.

❧ I approached my mom when I was six and asked, "When do I turn into a girl?" I was rushed into boys' sports and taught how to fish and hunt. I was told never to ask that question again.

❧ Another trans* person I knew. She understood my fears.

❧ My mother, and again I received a speech about what was expected of me.

❧ I was in a very bad marriage and because of that I tried to talk with a USAF mental health clinic. That resulted in my being outed to my commander. I had my security clearance pulled and was forced to retire from the Air Force. This was in Athens, Georgia, in 1985.

❧ My spouse.

❧ I first told my girlfriend when I was 17. She was not so put off by the idea but was not interested in helping me or discussing much.

❧ My doctor (late in my career). He put me on M2F hormones, but after a year and experiencing breast development and loss of libido, I quit them. After another year and seeing my doctor again, I started 16 years of taking testosterone to undo what had been done. It did not work. I then quit the "T" and after further consultations, I resumed my M2F hormone regimen.

❧ There was not a single moment. I started to realize what the things I had been saying meant. People were silent or did not understand what I was saying. I am not "out" about my aspirations beyond androgyny, yet.

❧   I innocently approached my mother at a very young age. Unfortunately, she was very conservative and strict. She was a seamstress, and when she was away one day, I made myself a beautiful skirt (having watched her many times, I had the necessary skill). I proudly showed it off to her when she returned. I went from pride to shame in 20 seconds! So much that it took 50 years to come back around.

❧   I broke down in my boyfriend's arms one night and told him that I was female to male (FTM). Luckily, my boyfriend was also FTM; so he figured I was, too, and is very supportive. He understands that it is newer for me than for himself and is extremely helpful when I have questions or when I am scared.

❧   I chose not to tell anyone for like 36 years. Then I approached a professional therapist for help in dealing with it. She dealt with me with compassion and understanding.

❧   I spoke to my partner about it at the time. She was ambivalent. She had "a lot of things" going on in her own life, and suggested that I speak to a mutual trans man friend of ours.

❧   For me, confusion is not a good word. I do not feel I was ever confused. I can remember as a kid sitting and putting a hand on each side of my chest pushing in to create cleavage with anticipation of what one day I would have. The first person that I openly spoke to about it was a friend that knew if I were asked a question, I would answer it honestly and without shame. I was 15 and he was 16. I have on occasion talked with a younger brother of mine about life growing up. He would say that I was always in your face with directness and never any shame. I was not ashamed.

❧   I very first approached my best friend's Aunt Megan; she is MTF (Male to Female). She explained to me her situation and why I was okay. She told me, "It will take time, but you'll become yourself. One day."

✤   My fiancé. Acceptance at first, as she thought it was a passing thing. She convinced me to go to therapy. I told her she might not like the results. We are no longer engaged or friends. She could not handle the truth.

✤   When I came out and finally told that I was gay and transgender, it was to my mother, which did not turn out as I planned it. Her already accepting that I was gay was so-so and on the edge. But to find out that her only son was transgender, well let's just say that is where I lost my mom; that is when my family turned their backs on me. My mother had her own dreams for my life, but her dreams were not mine. So she told me to get out of her house and never set foot back in her door. So I had no choice but to walk out her door and say goodbye.

✤   Well, sexual orientation did not enter the picture for a long time. My concern had to do with my gender identity.

⚜ My grandma. She told me it was disgusting and wrong. I handled it like any other child would. I stayed quiet and let her criticize me until she was finished.

⚜ I would have to say my mother. It really was not handled. No one really knew what to do. Both of my parents, family, teachers and clergy tried everything they could to convince me otherwise.

⚜ It was my mom who, surprisingly, already knew at eighteen. I had already preferred dating women, and she had me watch a talk show at sixteen about being trans, which kind of got the wheels turning for me. I had a name for how I felt, and I was not alone anymore.

⚜ Doctor told my parents, "Your child will grow out of it."

⚜ I told no one.

⚜ The first person I spoke to about my sexual orientation was my grandmother. I told her that I felt like a boy and liked girls. My grandmother told me that she knew I was different and no matter what I would always be her grandchild. She told me that she loved me unconditionally and would be there for me no matter what. She promised to never tell anyone, per my request. She kept her promise and literally took the secret to her grave. She passed away the same year.

⚜ I came out to an online friend literally about a year or so ago about how I was feeling, and instead of support, they suggested that I might just not be happy with how fat I was and suggested I exercise to see if that got rid of what I was feeling. It hurt me a lot and delayed my coming out. Then a good girlfriend I was living with at the time. I was 19.

⚜ My mom; she kind of ignored it.

Chapter Four

What single term is most acceptable to define transgender or transitioning people?

"Yes, we should not have to define each other."

➤ "Transgender." However, this does become a past identity for some post-transition who may go on to simply identify as male or female. For me personally, I will always identify as transgender, no matter how far into or past my transition I may be.
➤ Transgender
➤ Transsexual
➤ Trans Folk
➤ People
➤ Human
➤ The pronoun that defines their presenting gender
➤ Trans
➤ Trans-woman/Trans-man
➤ Genderlicious
➤ T-trapped
➤ Trans* (with the asterisk)
➤ If one dresses as a female, then call them by that origin such as female, woman, lady, or girl. The same applies to ones that dress as males.
➤ Re-gendering

Chapter Five

In the beginning, which person became your best ally?

"Some of my best allies were other trans people I talked to online who had been through what I was going through. This is not to say I had no support from the people my "real life" -- but no one can understand what a trans person goes through like another trans person, and those willing to talk to me and give me advice became my strength to be patient with those in my everyday life who were working to understand."

⚜ I reached out to old high school classmates I had not spoken to in over 20 years. Two cis women befriended me and helped me move forward.

⚜ There was none. Not unless you count sensationalized reports in magazines. April Ashley, Coccinelle, and famous Christine Jorgensen.

⚜ My spouse.

⚜ My first wife was my best ally in the beginning. She would help me find and buy clothing shoes and makeup. At first, she never shamed me or made me feel guilty but grew tired of my wanting to express my female persona.

⚜ My live-in spouse. She was aware of my breasts and my propensity for wanting to be female. She told me to be just me. Two years after we got together, I started on M2F hormones (second time). Two years later I shaved off my beard (had worn one to mask my femininity for over 22 years). I then "came out" to family and many friends but never came out to my professional associates. I was retired; so this was easy. I quit all the professional fraternities I belonged to and literally began a new life.

⚜ A girlfriend because I could not detect any desire in her for me to be masculine.

⚜ The beginning in this case is 56 years old: I met my wonderful partner via the virtual world Second Life. My avatar in-world was female. After becoming best friends and before proceeding further, I came out. It took a bit for her to recover from the deception, but she saw the true me. We met in real life and have been together ever since. We will be married in 2 months. Being an ally in this case is not unconditional support but rather the give and take and questioning and doubting and holding my feet to the fire. She came right with me on the journey, all the ups and downs.

⚜ I really would have to say my gender therapist is my closest ally. I do not have to lie or pretend when I am around her. She provides sound advice and helps me to deal with my fears.

⚜ My friend Luke, who had been a friend through entertaining for several years and who had also begun to transition a few years earlier than me. He was just far enough ahead of me to be able to confidently tell me what to expect and a good confidant with whom to discuss my feelings and experiences.

⚜ Myself. Through my family's un-excepting of anything other than the "norm," it was taught that you should never be ashamed of who you are if you are not doing anything wrong, and you would know it was wrong if you could not look yourself in the mirror. That told me that I was the one who knew if something for me was right or not. I am sure someone is regretting teaching me that idea growing up. The thing is, that I never ever feared those around me while growing up. I never had a bad experience in the community until I was well into my 40's and was called names by a group of youths.

❧   My brother Randy. He has always accepted me for me and adapted to me being his baby brother in a heartbeat. He and his soon-to-be wife are amazing, and I know that when they have kids, they are going to be great parents because they are the most accepting people in the world.

❧   Allies stand up for you as well as support you. I have not had anybody stand up for me that I know of. I do that for myself.

❧   I do not think I have had an ally yet. I have been outed to strangers by "friends" and I have had "friends" refuse to acknowledge me as a person in transition. I have had my ex-husband try to out me to my family during fights, I have been told I am not allowed to be who I am by some family members, and I have been told I will never be loved because of who I am.

❧   My fiancé. Always has been and likely will always be my biggest pillar of strength on this journey.

❧   My first ally was when I was in my forties. She owned a wig shop and understood that I was battling my own self for identity.

❧   The same trans* friend I confided in.

❧   My partner, who accepted and supported me completely pre-surgery and all during my transition and our marriage.

❧   My best friend for fourteen years. We have been friends since before my wife died of cancer. She is a GG [genetic girl] and straight. Only interested in men. She has supported me through all the trials and tribulations and in the general public eye. She hired me to be her Production Manager and put me right out there in the mix and in the public eye with her. Her friends told her she was nuts and no one would take me seriously. I am now a respected person in the community and have helped her career immensely. She is also now my roommate. We watch out for each other. Without her, I would have been lost.

❧   The person that became my best ally was my high school friend, Olga. She has always known about my lifestyle, and I never had to tell her. She is the one who stood by me even to this day. The first time she ever saw me as a woman, she looked at me and said, "There's my girlfriend. I have been waiting for you." I was in shock because she was so accepting of who I was and never cared what I looked like. To this day, she stands tall and proud of who I became in life after what my family did to me. My best friend became my family. Her love for me is unconditional; she is my family.

❧   My best ally was an MTF I met in an online support group. Within a year, we were married.

❧   My best friend, Stefan Delgado. We have a mutual understanding as friends. And my choice in lifestyle does not affect him.

❧   My sister. She supported me, and it was her I turned to when I finally accepted what I should have known since childhood but hid because of shame and fear.

❧   My mom and my best friend. They supported my decision, and they believed in me. My family has faced many things, and that support kept me alive when I would be dead.

❧   Beaumont Society and their local representative. She is transgender and understood my intersex condition.

❧   A very dear friend who was a police dispatcher in Ft Worth Texas. Well, I had a grandmother that knew. She was not happy about it, but she never told my folks. I came out to a campus minister. He was not really sure how to deal with it. He told me to seek further counseling.

❧   My friend Richard and also my friend Carrie. Both are 110% supportive and wonderful people. Richard helped push me to come out to my husband when I did. Carrie has kept me on that path and listened to every word I have had to say. They are amazing, and I could not have asked for better people to stand by my side.

❧   My girlfriend; she makes everything easier.

Chapter Six

In the beginning, which important person in your life became your worst hater/detractor?

"My then-wife was unable to accept my gender variance."

❦ My oldest son. Turns out he is an extreme homophobe due to an incident that occurred in school when he was young. Unfortunately, he will not listen or research anything and will not contact me or return any of my outreaches. He has confused gender and sexuality and will not reconcile. Also unfortunately, he is the father of my two grandsons.

❦ I think hater is the wrong word. Worst critic would be a married woman with her own problems that she refuses to deal with. She started out wanting to be a friend but had worked at my school. However, in the end she started calling me woman to my face and to others on campus, and said not to force my beliefs on her. She had confided in me prior that she had strict parents who forced her to marry the person to whom she gave her virginity. She divorced after years of abuse but because divorce was a sin, married again and justified all this, yet told me she knew she was a lesbian.

❦ My entire family. Growing up, my family used to tell me to go up to complete strangers and say obscenely rude things to them because of their gender identity or sexual orientation. Being all of about five, I had no idea what the words I was saying meant. Looking back now, I realize that was not only abusive towards complete strangers, but that was also highly abusive towards my own psyche.

✤ Both parents, especially my father when he was given a pair of tights found by my mother. They accused me of being gay. My father threatened to send me off to military school. He beat me, too, of course. I guess I would have to say my parents, both of them. My Father probably , then subsequent girlfriends. I told the girl friends it enhanced our sex lives.

✤ I cannot think of one person that has done anything to make themselves considered a "hater" by any means. Everyone in my life (aside from my father), to my surprise, has been fully supportive.

✤ My Mother. I was born intersex. Not the perfect child. To her I as imperfect and a disgrace.

✤ No-one has become a hater; however, I am not fully out to all friends and family.

✤ I do not recall anyone who fit this. The few people I ever told that knew me before were neither surprised nor not supportive. Most people wondered why I had not done it sooner.

✤ My brother. My little brother was a confidant and I had disclosed my GID diagnoses to him. He seemed fine with it, but four months later when I told him I was going to transition he told me, "You do whatever the hell you want to do, but if that is what you are going to do, we are through with you."

✤ A neighbor who tried to kick in my door at 1 am while screaming that I was a faggot and demanding I come out so that he could kill me.

✤ I have not experienced hate, just confusion.

✤ My best male friend from early childhood found out about when I got dressed-up when visiting a group of girlfriends and tormented me later during my teens. I hated being in the restroom because he would make a huge scene when I tried to sit to pee.

❦   I knew my mother would never accept me, and I would have never come out while she was alive.

❦   A girlfriend. She would make exaggerated disapproving comments about gay or transgender people, obviously for my benefit, at moments when I did not demonstrate fear of looking or acting feminine. Because of that, I hid my thoughts from her and did not continue cross-dressing.

❦   Well, right after I came out, I had moved in with my boyfriend. However, I lost every chance at a relationship with my dad. My dad and I were extremely close when I was younger, but he started owning a business, and he lost a relationship with the entire family. Eventually my dad built up a relationship with my siblings, but still refuses to talk to me due to my life choices.

❦   I still hide myself from most people in real life. Sad, I know but necessary for now. I have yet to deal with major amounts of criticism or outright hated except through the media. I have tested many of my friends and found them unaccepting of people that are gay, lesbian or trans.

❦   When I finally began to transition, my partner of four plus years said she would be "supportive," and I believed her. It turned out she was anything but. She had identified as a lesbian, but began cheating on me with a cisgendered (biological) man. We broke up shortly thereafter, and she went on to say, I should "never have tried to be a man." I think in all honesty she merely did not like it when the attention was taken off her. She admitted as much, but I used to think she was kidding. She was not.

❦   It was only later in life I could define anyone as a hater. Those people were either females being females or men that did not get the freak show they thought they were going to get.

❦   My worst hater would have to be my ex-best friend, Brit. She told me numerous times that I would always be a girl until I have bottom surgery. She led me on in the dating field   and right as we would get close, reminded me that she is "straight" and being with me would make her bi.

❦   My former fiancé; talking constantly behind my back while being nice to me in public.

❦   My worst hater in my life is my baby sister. She gave me all of her gowns after she graduated from high school. She was Homecoming Queen, and the gown she wore was the gown I received my first crown. After that, all of her little girlfriends started giving me their gowns and dance outfits. I felt like I was on cloud nine. Thanks to my baby sister and her friends, I had a great start in gowns and dance outfits.

❦   There was no one who hated me at all, or else I just did not even realize it.

❦   My Grandma. I did what any other child would do. I stayed quiet and let her criticize me until she was finished.

❦   My closest friend.

❦   My grandma is a Jehovah's Witness. She would not use my legally changed name, used the wrong pronouns, and just made me question if this is who I really am.

❦   Two social workers who split up my family. They saw transsexualism as a perversion and not normal and thought that my children would grow up gay or trans if they were left in my care.

❦   I do not really have too much negativity right now dealing with my coming out and my trans*, but the silence I have gotten from some of my family hurts me deeper than any negative words could. The silence, ignoring the elephant in the room. That hurts a great deal to me.

❦   My father, who removed himself from my life.

Chapter Seven

How did you handle criticism of the first person to express hatred?

"Why get or stay angry? If they do not experience it themselves, how can they understand? I let them go and any feelings I had about it. The passage of time shows them the reality of what I am."

⚜   I was not angry with anyone. My then-wife was very angry with me.

⚜   Since I knew she had personal problems stemming from too strict parental upbringing, where they needed to look good so they wanted her to do things to gain praise, I knew her bullying me was because she could not bear to accept who she is and love herself as she really is. I called her on it, as I am blunt. She was in denial, but admitted some things. In the end, she and her husband chose to isolate themselves. They not only do not speak to me, they always sit alone in the cafeteria. I feel bad for her, as she needs to love herself before she can help others as a social worker to be.

⚜   I ignored it for a long time. I was young and just trying to survive in the "home" I had to go home to. Even now, I ignore it. I need an education so that I can better myself and help others. I deal with the anger and self-loathing on my own time, but I suck it up at "home."

⚜   Silence. Besides hostility, I drank, did drugs, alcohol, illicit drugs, sniffing lacquer thinner at work.

❧   I became withdrawn and quiet. I felt unwanted, and so I crawled into reading and being anti-social as not letting people become friends with me.

❧   The only way you can handle a person who turns their back on you. You walk away.

❧   That night, I called the police, who took him down to the station for the night. I slept at a friend's that night and had a borrowed gun next to the bed. The next day when I was talking to the landlord the neighbor was let out. Before going to his apartment, he started right up again. He was evicted.

❧   I tried to fight back once. I got hit and pushed in the shower. After that I found ways to avoid the boys locker room.

❧   In school, I was not accepted and was beat on whenever I left myself in a vulnerable position. An elderly man living next door always called me "Roberta." One day I got cornered by a gang of boys, and they forced me to fight them. I did my best and made it hard for them. While I did not win, they got the message that I was tenacious and would not give up. My neighbor saw this and never called me Roberta again. This made a lasting impression on me and became the foundation of a persona (alter ego) that I would hide behind for most of my life. It even led to me becoming a Captain of icebreakers.

❧   I was overloaded with hatred for almost everything about me. So, it is hard to say when the first time was. When it was directly about gender role issues, I was defiant and shut them up by not acting ashamed.

❧   I kept calm and held the 'high' road. Attempting to explain until I saw that he would not listen -- he was physically shaking. I got up, said goodnight and left. I send cards and presents to him and his family and will continue to do so. Nothing has come back this way. I only know what is happening from his mother (my ex) and my other son.

⚜ I was not necessarily mad or angry; I was hurt. My dad meant everything to me; so to have him pretty much completely walk out of my life made me upset. I do not cry often, but every now and then, it hits me that I cannot just pick up my phone and call him because he would just reject it. I even refused to talk to my sister because she did not stand up for me, but I realized that she cannot control him and that I had to get over that. I did try to hide it from his side of the family, but my happiness was more important than his acceptance.

⚜ I have tried to slowly educate my friend on mental health and LGBT issues as a way to plow the road for when I come out as Trans.

⚜ I actually ceased transition for about 8 months -- the period of time I had hoped to win her back. Pretty gross decision in retrospect. Glad I got over her.

⚜ I felt bad for their thinking they felt they needed to react critically of anything. That is usually something that you are taught by having had it done to you, or you had learned as a way of harming another.

⚜ I bottled it all up. I did not know what else to do; so I would bottle it up and self-harm. I HATED being misgendered and for every misgender by my family or close friends, I would self-harm.

⚜ I let it be; it is not my fault they are angry. At first, I did not understand how they could be angry then, but they were born in a different time, and over the years, she has come around but still not completely.

⚜ Eating disorders, cutting myself, and self-harm.

⚜ I would write my family members letters to let them know how I felt about how I am as a person and the way I was being treated for being different. I stated that I did not ask to be this way just as I did not ask to have them as a family, yet it turned out that way. I stated that I will always be related to them and love them no matter what. I let them know that I will give them time to come to terms. At times, I am still angered that I am not fully accepted as a male, yet I came to terms that it is their choice just as I had made mine.

✤   I am dealing with my family's silence day by day. My aunt has brought tears to my eyes because she is been a wonderful support and voice against the rest of my family who have stayed silent towards me. So far, I am just rolling with what I am getting and remembering I do have wonderful support where it is needed.

✤   Not well. I was extremely angry and hurt to the point of my hurting myself.

✤   I sat them down and explained to my best ability the whys and how's of things. One key point in all my conversations was to point out it was a birth defect, not a choice. I have changed many stout Christian beliefs and have brought hard-core Bible thumpers to my side with their support.

✤   In the beginning, I handled my anger very well. I had my days when I just cried because the ones important to me were always the ones that hurt me. So from there, my anger got worse. I would cuss them, and I would make them feel as low as they made me feel. I would pull up things in their life to hurt them the way they hurt me. In the beginning, it was all about paybacks. My anger turned me into a person I no longer knew anymore. I still stayed in their lives but made them feel the same hurt that they showed me.

✤   I made my feelings numb and my mind desensitized.

✤   I cried a lot and drifted away from them. I just started questioning whether they ever were truly friends.

Chapter Eight

In the beginning, how did you handle any anger towards less important or unimportant people in your life?

"They are less important people for a reason, right? I know it is easier said than done, but I just had to realize that they could not control my life; so why let them get to me? At first, I was upset at every little thing people said, and I just held it in, but I learned that I had to let go. I started writing a lot, just something every day in a book just to let out some anger or feelings."

❧ With a live and let live attitude, also called resignation.

❧ Just breathe.

❧ Sometimes I would cry, other times I would try to do petty harmful things to get back at them, when possible.

❧ I avoided people who did not like me or whom I felt uncomfortable with.

❧ Anger in the third person? From as far back as I can remember, I have been fiercely defensive of other people being treated badly. It is much easier for me to defend others than to defend myself.

❧	Consoled with my allies, mostly at work, but also with my partner. In many cases, my allies took action behind my back to mitigate situations. I am very fortunate.

❧	I tried to slowly educate my friend on mental health and LGBT issues as a way to plow the road for when I come out as Trans.

❧	I get angry for twenty minutes like a good Italian, and then I forget about it.

❧	I think the word "anger" is a word being used to hype up a situation. If a word had to be used, why not anxiety? Maybe it is the whole if you can look yourself in the mirror thing growing up, but anger is usually a defensive reaction. My anxiety over intolerance by others was in fact a way of questioning how what I was doing could cause them inconvenience.

❧	Humor, and trying not to let them get too embarrassed by mistaking my gender.

❧	I shrugged it off. They did not matter to me because I knew who I was.

❧	Ignored it after trying to explain and then telling them it is your right to think the way you wish as long as you do not act violently on it.

❧	In the beginning, my anger towards non- significant people in my life was not so good. I went as low as to fight, or cuss them down, which got me nowhere. I started seeing myself changing for the worse. I became a very mean and hateful person. I started questioning the person that I was becoming, which turned me into a person who stopped caring about anything. I started hanging with the wrong crowd, which made me turn to drugs to deal with everyday life. Drugs took over the person that I first became. I would get drugged up and head to the bars, where I did more drugs.

❀   I stayed quiet and let them criticize me, or I just walked away.

❀   Held my head high, corrected their mistaken gendered comments, and walked away. It was interesting that when I started living full time, I became confident and stronger as a person than I would ever been.

❀   I got upset, but I let it go. It is not my burden to carry; I do not have a problem. If it was something I could not ignore, I would try to educate them. Everyone is human.

❀   I hid away and turned the anger inside myself.

❀   I began to withdraw from anyone. I did solitary hobbies. I had a way too short temper. Drinking, smoking building hotrods, building plastic models, stealing clothes off clothes lines.

❀   I ignored those people who were non-significant to me. At first I would be angered by their hatred and would write out my feelings on paper and then burn the paper.

❀   It hurt badly. I would take it personally.

❀   If someone called me SHE/HER or my birth name, often I corrected them angrily. I would be focused on that for the rest of the day or weekend.

❀   I ignored it.

❀   I learned to let people's thoughts or actions towards me not bother me or at least not let them know they had hurt me.

❀   Actually, for me, those less important people had a very large impact. I found out who comprised my hate groups. Anger against me was underhanded at work. They made life miserable; so I left.

Chapter Nine

What is the worst thing someone did to hurt you emotionally as you transitioned?

"My husband at the time kept threatening to leave. Finally, I left him. Now that he is my ex-husband, he says he is still in love with me, and wants us to "spend as much time together as a couple" before I decide to finish transitioning. I believe love is unconditional, and I do not want a partner who will bail on me because parts of my body have changed...that is NOT love."

❧ Repeated these bible passages: Deuteronomy 22:5 King James Version (KJV) *The woman shall not wear that which pertaineth unto a man, neither shall a man put on a woman's garment: for all that do so are abomination unto the Lord thy God.* Leviticus 18:22 King James Version (KJV) *Thou shalt not lie with mankind, as with womankind: it is abomination.*

❧ My closest friend told me that no matter what I did, HRT (hormone replacement therapy), surgeries, anything, I would always be a man. I was born male, and nothing would ever change that. I tried to explain, but he just insisted I was a man. I cried for weeks.

❧ Said she would not stay with me.

⚜ I have had people stop talking to me, call me names, make fun of me to where I just stopped going to public places since I was not seen as my true self. It can really break you down not having emotional support.

⚜ Took my children away and convinced their daughter (my former partner) that she was straight and not bisexual.

⚜ Making me feel like I was some sort of freak, a child molester, a gay man, someone no one wanted to be a friend. Rejection, walking out of my life.

⚜ I was an abomination and tell me I should be stoned to death. They turned other family members against me by forcing them to choose between the two of us. Unfortunately, it was my big sister.

⚜ My girlfriends told me I was ugly and that I was akin to a gay man even though I wanted nothing to do with men. My now ex-wife would always be telling me how horribly I dressed.

⚜ As I said, so far it is the silence from people. The less communication now that I am out and male. I had many heterosexual male friends, and now a lot of them seemed to just fall by the wayside. It feels emotionally like the brick wall I had around me is crumbling.

⚜ Name calling and hurtful comments.

⚜ Probably the worst thing was an arrogant guy introducing me to three men in the cafeteria and then blurting out in American Sign Language that I had a clit and small dick. "Too Much Information," was what one said, shocked. Actually what may hurt worse though was when a former best friend of a decade said God cannot use my being transgender; the devil caused it. We used to talk online often; she hardly ever talks at all now. She had suggested I marry her brother in law, but now I bet she does not even want me to visit her and her family in India.

⚜ I feel the worst thing would be to turn your back on

someone you once claimed to love just because they are now happy.

❧ The person told me they were leaving me and taking my daughter with them. She kept my daughter hidden for four months.

❧ I cannot recall anyone doing this.

❧ My ex-wife. She refused to talk to me ever again. This was a hard hit, too, because she was my best friend for sixteen years.

❧ I called the police on a neighbor who, very high, tried to kick in my door one night at 1 am. He was totally insane. He was screaming that I was a faggot and had AIDS, all the time kicking and punching the door. He was arrested. I slept at a friend's that night and kept a borrowed revolver next to the bed. When released the next day he picked up right where he stopped. He was evicted the next day.

❧ People who say gender just does not matter.

❧ My ex-wife outed me to all my family and friends before I was ready and then abandoned me.

❧ I was shunned by my motorcycle chapter and threatened they would beat me if we should ever cross paths.

❧ The worst was not direct and not a single incident. One episode was my mother and another person talking to each other, obviously for my benefit, about gay people being unloving and perverse. That is indirectly related to my gender related thoughts and feelings.

❧ My son's rejection of me, which continues to grate. This also cuts off my access to my two beautiful grandchildren and to a wonderful daughter-in-law.

❧ The woman who knew I loved her cheating on me; that hurt the most.

❀   It was a friend that did not think they could say, "Girl you are missing the mark, you might want to reconsider that look." It is like letting your Grandmother walk down the street with toilet paper on her shoe.

❀   My closest friend in the world made me think she was completely okay with everything for years and years and then turned around. I found out she had been calling me my birth name and lying about everything to me. I miss her most, but she will never come around; so I will live without her.

❀   When people do not take me seriously, it hurts more than direct hate. If someone tells me being trans is wrong or against the Bible or whatever the case may be, I can brush it off as just another ignorant hater, but it is when someone makes a comment about "Well you are not REALLY trans because..." or "You are trying to get attention..." or "You cannot be feminine sometimes and still call yourself a transman…" it gets to me like a splinter under my skin.

❀   My former fiancé told my daughter before I could tell her. Subsequently it backfired on my fiancé, and my daughter and I have become closer.

❀   The worst thing someone did to hurt me emotionally was done by my baby sister. After she graduated from high school, she got married and had three beautiful children: two girls and a boy, just like my mom did, and being who and what I am, she stopped me from talking to them or even seeing them. I have a niece I have never laid eyes on, and she is now turning eight years old. My baby sister did not want me near her children or to speak to them so she did not have to explain why their uncle looked like a girl. I was a disgusting, and nasty person in her and her husband's eyes.

❀   It was ten years after I transitioned that a family member said he "related transgenderism to pedophilia and wife-swapping."

Chapter Ten

What is the worst thing someone did to hurt you physically (not emotionally) as you transitioned?

✤ Had hobbies taken from me, and being beaten.

✤ I did not have any physical contact because of my transition.

✤ Gay men in a gay bar beat me up and told me never to come back. They stated, "These are our men and we do not need your type around confusing them."

✤ Being kicked in the belly.

✤ Nothing bad has happened.

✤ Since my beginning transition, I have had no physical abuse.

✤ My transition never resulted in any physical violence, just threats.

✤ I am not "out" about transforming. Being raped by a stranger was related to being effeminate.

✤ Has not been a problem, luckily.

✤ So far nothing.

✤ When my ex broke up with me, I had to move out of her house. I was hurt financially, which is somewhat physically.

Luckily, that is the worst as of this moment.

❧   No none has ever hurt me physically due to my transitioning.

❧   Physically hurt, was my dad who molested me and beat me. My dad always told me that I would get it and get it good. His beatings where the worst, and after he beat me, he would lock me in a chicken wire bird cage that he built to breed white doves in the garage. I would be in there for hours. After the family had dinner, he would let me out, and I had to eat dinner out in the garage because my stepmother was cleaning up the kitchen. Also after confiding in whom I thought would be an understandable human. The same person I confided in was accepting about my choice, but he had another agenda. To him I was just pussy. He kept asking to have sex with me. I kept declining his requests; so he tried to take me by force. We physically fought until he overcame me raped me.

❧   I got pretty lucky, did not get beat up or anything. Had a few threats they would cut my head off or kill me but that is it.

❧   Raped by my former partner.

❧   The worst thing someone did to physically hurt me was hit the back of my knees with a bat to make me drop to the ground, rape me, and then punch me in the face multiple times, which gave me a concussion and made my tooth go through my cheek.

❧   Nothing so far psychically has taken place. I am going to hope that it never does. I hope it does not happen to other people as well.

❧   Punched me and beat me up.

❧   Strangled and threatened me with a knife on multiple occasions.

Chapter Eleven

Top 20
Most Offensive Words

1. Tranny

2. Shemale
3. Freak
4. Faggot
5. Sex-change
6. Having a mental breakdown
7. Sissy
8. Sexist
9. Gay
10. Fag
11. Queer
12. Change
13. Transvestite
14. PASSING!
15. Genitals
16. Female
17. Male
18. Not a real man
19. Not a real women
20. It

Why do you consider the words from the list above to be offensive?

❧   Because it is a dirty slang word most used by transgender haters and enemies to describe how they see a transgender male or female.

❧   Passing means that I am pretending well.

❧   Everyone wants to know what's in my pants when it is no one's business. A penis does not make the man; his heart and actions do.

❧   I am a woman in my heart soul and emotionally.

❧   This word is derogatory, and comes from pornography. It is not a word from the medical field, nor a term used to describe accurately anyone in the trans spectrum. The sole purpose is to mock and lower the person to less than human status. It is akin to NIGGER and POLLOCK and HOMO. It is nothing but a word to bully, and make it okay to bully. It is not a term of endearment such as DEAFIE is to the Deaf.

❧   'Tranny' is a word the porn industry came up with to oppress transgender people. It spread, and now people think it is okay to call people a Tranny. I think it is highly disrespectful and unbelievably rude.

❧   I work hard to be a woman of class and upbringing. I choose my outfits carefully, and I dress like the women I see on television news and those in legal professions. Defining me as some trailer trash bitch is a low blow.

Publisher's Note: No implication allows replacing one derogatory term with another, such as trailer trash.

❧   People transitioning are never less human than another person is. They are not freaks any more than you are or I am. They need love and friendship, not hatred

❧   It is a slur used primarily in the porn/sex industry. I am not and never will be a child of the porn/sex industry, and I very much dislike the parallel that people seem to draw between transgendered people and porn/sex.

❧   I do not equate being a male to female individual as a gay or lesbian individual, and only ignorant people would use such hurtful words.

❧   The term infers that birth sex and gender are the same thing and is often taken to include sexuality.

❧   It is based in porn, as if sex had anything to do with transition.

❧   Those outside our world think that these people represent us. They also focus their attention to male parts, ignoring our existence in the real world.

❧   My sex (i.e. genitals) may or may not change; my gender is changing.

❧   I feel it is my gender identity and not my sexuality that I am expressing.

❧   I consider myself of sound mind. When I tried to renew my gun licenses, I was put through a grueling process by the RCMP, and my doctors and background were thoroughly checked in spite of the fact that I used weapons throughout my military career. It was demeaning.

❧   It identifies me with people who cross-dress because some think it is humiliating to be female and enjoy being humiliated.

❧   I am not a freak or a pervert; I am just misunderstood. I always thought I should have been born a girl

❧   It offends me, since I see myself as a man.

❧	It sounds like an offensive slang word. I know that is not always the case, but it feels wrong to me to be used. Maybe because it has been used as a bad word in the past.

❧	It just adds to my dysphoria.

❧	Based on ignorance, phobias, and deep-seated wish to not be enlightened.

❧	It brings to mind a bad Jerry Springer episode that is there only to shock "normal people" for ratings.

❧	The word sex makes one thing of sex organs. Being transgender has A LOT more to it than just sex.

❧	Because seeing myself as a woman who likes men the same as other women do should not define me as what two men who like each other are. I do not like labels anyway, but keep it logical.

❧	I am not changing. Change is something you do to make yourself different. I am not making myself different. I am becoming the man society never allowed me to be before.

❧	To me, this word created back in the early 1900's and popularized by Hollywood is tantamount to using the "N" word.

❧	Faggot is a word that does not stand right with me. That is a word that will bring out an evil side of me. Yes, that word is used every day to so many others. The word faggot is a racist word in my eyes, just like the "N" word. Being called a faggot is the lowest blow any gay or transgendered person could be called. It is very hurtful, and whoever calls you that also could be a dangerous person. I have had friends killed by people who called them faggots. So this is why the evil side of me comes out when I hear that word.

❧	It is an old term for homosexual cross dressers.

Chapter Twelve

Describe your feelings about transgendered entertainers performing in "drag shows."

"I think it is great that they can do that. As long as you enjoy what you are doing, I will never judge you. It may not be my cup of tea, but that does not matter. Be you; be proud."

⚜ I love it. If that is what you want to do, more power to you. Gender bending in any form is marvelous, and having the courage to play with gender before, during, or after transitioning is something that should be encouraged.

⚜ I do not know much about that. Growing up I almost always was in a dress, a boy in drag. If this is a transman dressed in a dress, it really is not much of a show, as we all do that. I figure if I do it for my school drag event, it will just confuse everyone about what gender I really want to be identified as; so I think I will not. As an actor, I really would not mind doing it on a stage if they did not know me.

⚜ A bunch of immature assholes making a great deal out of nothing and hurling their hatred towards women in general. They are gay men acting like immature jerks.

⚜ I think that if they are okay with who they are and that they enjoy what they are doing, then go for it.

⚜ I am okay with it. Drag shows at one time were an art

form of entertainment. A few straight men do drag. If a transgender does drag to make money, then it is her business, not mine.

❖ Whilst they should be viewed purely as entertainers, unfortunately often they are not so viewed. Instead, some members of general society consider them typical of trans* people. That can create concerns regarding acceptance.

❖ Usually entertaining.

❖ First of all, more power to them. They are having fun, enjoying themselves, and practicing art. I am a little worried that this tends to solidify some of the stereotypes cis-normative people have and tends to make it harder to explain what I am (transsexual).

❖ I myself am a transgender entertainer who performs as a drag king or male illusionist. While unlike the traditional idea of a drag king, I am technically not a woman dressing as a man. I am still someone who was raised and socialized as a woman. I was not conditioned in the ways of dressing and acting "masculine," who now portrays a character that both highlights and questions what masculinity is. For me, it is not just about looking male on stage; it is about the art of costuming, performance, theatrics, and audio and visual entertainment. I think people get hung up on technicalities of these labels instead of focusing on the beauty behind the art and culture of drag, not to mention the fact that trans pioneers have paved the way for those drag shows to exist openly today.

❖ Drag performers are another hate group of nonsupport and open ire that I detest, and so I stay away from them. Their antics in open society give the world a very wrong idea and impression of what transition is all about. I hate that a gay man with a clothing and make up fetish can be under the same psychological umbrella as me, a person who for seven years prior to transition got physically ill every time I looked at my image in the mirror.

❖ Dislike. Unfortunately the bigots cannot understand the difference and think that they represent the entire gender community.

With their exaggeration, queens also mock women - cis and trans.

⚜   Brilliant.

⚜   I enjoy watching them, and find it entertaining. I have even participated doing the same as entertainment earlier in life just to get a chance to express my female persona. It is not what I am about, but if that is someone's thing, then let them do it.

⚜   I have no problem with true a truly transgender person performing in a drag show. What I do not like is gay men impersonating as drag queens.

⚜   This could be referring to many different things. The most interesting to me is probably that I feel alienated to some extent, because the woman that I am trying to be is beautiful, sweet, and strong. She is not interested in appearing like a prostitute but is not repulsed. It is just not interesting. Other thoughts are positive. I feel more comfortable in that environment than in an office.

⚜   I have no problem with this at all. Transition is expensive, way too expensive. A girl has to have a way to make good money for it.

⚜   I can appreciate it. I think that eventually most transgendered entertainers will have a platform of their own, but in the meantime, why stop people from entertaining who wish to entertain? I am transgendered -- born in a female body and taking hormones, but in order to perform as a man I still have to bind my 40 DD's to my back with duct tape, spray adhesive and a prayer, shadow my chest and stomach with makeup, use make up on my face, glue theatrical hair to my face, create awesome and expensive costumes, etc, etc. I am still creating an "illusion" in order to perform as a male -- hence, I am a Male Illusionist.

⚜   Anyone can be an entertainer. For me, I gave it up because it was not something that was fun anymore, and it helped me to represent that I was not trying to be someone an illusion, but be myself. It was a personal choice for me.

✤ I think it is good. Kids need to know that there are people out there that do that. It is okay. I never had that.

✤ I think drag is for fun and entertainment, and people should not be offended over whether transgender people should or should not participate. If a trans man wants to be a drag queen, let him. If a trans woman wants to be a drag queen, let her. People are going to disagree over what counts as drag as soon as anyone who is not cisgender gets involved. But why does anyone care?

✤ They have every right to perform and most of them performed drag prior to transition. Why should they not be allowed to perform in their art form just because they found their true selves?

✤ My feeling of transgender entertainers performing in drag shows is awesome. A drag queen is an illusion of a female impersonator, and a transgender woman or man is a fantasy illusion entertainer. It gives a variety of illusions in the art of drag shows.

✤ I have no problem with the performers, but the media often portrays all of us as drag queens.

✤ I see queens and princesses as only entertainers, and not relatable to transgender kind in any way. WHY? Because queens and princesses as entertainers have a choice to wear those kinds of flashy clothes and makeup just to make money and have fun! Transgender males and females DO NOT HAVE A CHOICE! We do not do this to make money or have fun! We do this to become whole as a regular human being and to be regarded as such because as a female when we look into a mirror we only see a girl. And when others try to put us in a male's lifestyle, we know it is not who we really are. Even when naked, our bodies disgust us because we know we should have been born with a female's body instead of a male's body.

✤ Who cares?

❀   If that is what they love, let them. Everyone needs an outlet. Sometimes that is the only work available to us, sadly to say, unless we want to live in a gender box. I do not feel it is fair though [for trans people to do so], since FTMs and MTFs can walk in ready to perform.

❀   Drag queens put down gender variant individuals.

❀   There are a lot of beautiful divas out there.

❀   They do more to define ALL of us as immature money grubbing whores and slutty acting dressing wack jobs.

❀   I do not really have too many feelings on this. I think that some of it could be "less" exaggerated, but that is really it. I see it more as a means of expression and theater than anything; so I do not find it offensive as some might.

Chapter Thirteen

Can you explain a positive path to restoring family relationships lost or to maintaining family relationships during transition?

"Maintaining any relationship during transition requires an enormous amount of patience. I had to remind myself constantly that I had my entire life to wrap my head around my gender, whereas the people in my life were still shocked by this brand new revelation. I had to be patient while the shock wore off and they came around. I also had to give them time to grieve. To those we love, our transition can feel like enduring the death of the "us" they've always known and the birth of the "new us." That grieving process needs to be endured with patience and compassion."

❧ I have been able to maintain a relationship with my grandmother. I hope she can someday build a bridge back to the rest of my family.

❧ My family has never been close. I have been back east once since 1985. My niece and I are the closest emotionally. I cannot expect an email from any of those people unless something really special happens.

⚜ Time.

⚜ Helping others try to understand that there is more to gender than what is culturally accepted and that this not a new phase or passing fad.

⚜ Patience is necessity. Everyone says it is okay and offers support, and then you never hear from them again. Over time, sometimes a lot of time, some will truly accept and try to renew the friendship.

⚜ I cannot say anything at this time about restoring family relationships as I have not told everyone. For maintenance, it is important to talk often. If away at school, I suggest writing home and sending photos, or texting them, using your name to remind them. Speak about things besides transition, but do not shy away from it. Just let it be natural part of talking just like religion, politics and other things have been. They fear change, thinking the worst, and that they will lose whom they knew. If you keep in contact and they see you still are you, it will help them transition with you.

⚜ Sadly, I cannot.

⚜ The most positive path to follow is your heart. Be honest and open about your feelings and work things out together

⚜ Communication is key. Never lay blame, and try your best to keep calm and answer any questions they may have.

⚜ I believe books or pamphlets help. Telling them what is going on as the process takes place is helpful. Explaining one's own feelings in regards to why the transition is taking place. Not every family member is going to be accepting. Eventually they will but not right away.

⚜ A positive path can only be when there is a strong emotional inter-relationship. This is particularly critical in the case of partners, who may need to overcome the loss of a physical relationship.

⚜   I am sorry, but I did not have a family relationship to maintain. I was not close to my parents. I was gay, and my parents did not accept this.

⚜   I keep in touch with my son using every medium at my disposal. However, I pace my contacts carefully so as not to burden or overwhelm. I continue to do this even though I see nothing in return. I think it is important for him to know that I exist, I am real, I do love him, and that I will be here for him -- unconditionally (even though he has broken my heart like no one has ever done).

⚜   When I do well with this sort of thing, I am being compassionate toward those whose are having problems with me and recognizing that, ultimately, I create my own emotions as they create theirs. The problems they are having represent dependence on an image of me that they have invented. I need to help them resolve their confusion. Love is responsibility without dependence. Compassion has no limit and no cost. So I am responsible but not at fault for their feelings. I am also responsible for my dependence on the image of them that I have invented. They are not at fault for my feelings.

⚜   Ho'omanawanui. The Hawaiian word for patience. It can take years.

⚜   Only thing I can think of would be to let time heal all wounds whether they be mental or physical.

⚜   That I was transitioning and that they were as well. I wanted understanding and acceptance and [realized] that they did too. For some, it took time, and I gave it. I also provided material for them to read. My family really wanted to know what took so long, and my mother's exact words were that she was happy to have her daughter back.

⚜   I learned to finally express myself, speak up to when I do not like something, like with my grandma. She sees my full beard yet still says "she." When I am around, the rest of my family looks at her like she is crazy saying the wrong things, not me.

⚜ No, I cannot, except for time.

⚜ Be kind, and give them time... but not too much time. You have to be firm in your needs. If you need your family to call you by your preferred name or pronouns, give them some time to get used to it but then start making it a black or white decision. It will make you feel better, and it will help them, too.

⚜ Be understanding of the ways different generations have been. Educate yourself about the past. Without empathy, you cannot expect understanding or change. Listen before you speak. Ask, before you answer. Do not anticipate reactions but welcome interaction. (You can quote me on that.)

⚜ I am still transitioning, and it is hard not knowing who's gonna be here tomorrow, but by not mentioning it to the people in my family who do not agree, it saves drama. It hurts knowing they do not [know], but it is great knowing they are still there.

⚜ Being totally honest and sitting down with them ready to answer any and all questions without getting offended by whatever they ask. If they do not accept you fully up front, allow them the time to adjust, all the time letting them know you are not angry with them and that you still and always will love them no matter. This method has worked with my entire family and with only one hold out -- my youngest brother -- and after four years now, he is starting to come around.

⚜ Restoring family relationships lost is a very slow process. Some may have their different ways of doing it. As for me, I stood back and let them come to me. Family has their own ways of coming back into your life. This does not happen overnight. It took years for me. And out of the blue, they came to me. See, we may not be what our family want us to be, but over the years of not being around for holidays, believe it or not you are the piece that has always been missing and that they try to get back to fill in the hole that is been empty for so long.

❦   Being yourself and having hope.

❦   Only time will tell.

❦   I am a parent to my son. I try and show him I am there at all times, both emotionally and physically for him

❦   Almost a week after going on HRT, my mood improved drastically and remained stable for the first time that I could remember in my life. Friends and family were asking, "What you are taking?" I would not give details. I only would say I had been given new medications after a lot of evaluation. They bought it.

❦   I think slow but gradual exposure to the issues surrounding transitions and education is a wonderful thing to try. Being up front and as open as you can be to your loved ones, who might feel lost or confused, is a great way to help.

Chapter Fourteen

Who was the most important person lost during transition that later came back on their own?

"I guess my wife. We are friends again, and that is good, as we have a fourteen-year-old son. He has both parents again."

❧   I did not really relate to this. My family is small. My uncle did not understand it, but he is trying, which is nice. He is a man of few words and just said to help him understand.

❧   Nobody lost has come back, but not many have been lost. Most of those that have been were let go by me, and I do not want those back.

❧   I guess my ex-wife. I think she saw where HRT was a very calming effect on my short temper.

❧   My father and I were estranged prior to transitioning. Open communication and time were the best things. Now that I know who my father has become, I can better understand what was wrong.

❧   I have not experienced that yet. My mom is not willing to accept. I would pray that she does, but that is still a stone unturned at this time.

❧   None.

❧   No one has come back.

❧ One of the couples who were closest when I was married to my ex-wife, initially acted shocked and disgusted, but since then our relationship has been re-established and remains open and enjoyable.

❧ A pilot friend was taken aback and would not speak to me after finding out about my transition. Later, he tried to befriend me, as his wife was totally accepting of me. Unfortunately, I could not go back and refused to renew what had been a lifetime friendship and professional relationship.

❧ My ex-wife. A number of things summed up to end our marriage; being transsexual was one of the underlying causes. Years after everything was said and done, she saw through the clutter to this issue of transsexualness. I think for her, it explained what happened and took the burden of guilt off of her. As she stated, "I never could have stayed married to you as a woman, but I see how we can now become very good girl friends."

❧ This has not happened to me yet; still in the closet.

❧ My brother. He is the only one that did not accept me fully and is now coming around. Unfortunately, I think the only thing that brought him around is the fact he has cancer, and he is seeing his own mortality now and that family, no matter what, is needed in life.

❧ The most important person in my life that I lost during transition is my mother. This question I really cannot answer because nothing has been restored and no walls have been brought down. But everyone's life is different.

❧ My grandma. Did not agree with my choice but later just put up with it.

❧ My younger sister. It was her faith that kept her from physically seeing me. I wrote her telling her that it was truly painfully not seeing her. She asked me questions about faith, and I gave her the answers she needed to hear. I did not believe what I said, but she needed to hear them. So for her I replied. Was it worth giving in? Yes.

⚜ My children, as they have been taught to hate me.

Chapter Fifteen

Do your parents refer to you as your documented birth sex, or do they now confirm your real gender?

Publisher's Note: I am surprised so many waited until the death of their parents to transition. Hopefully our world will change enough for people to live without hiding. It may not be in my life, but because of people like you, we are making the early steps with projects like this book.

"My father is good at calling me 'he'. He said, 'If Cher can do it, so can I.' My mother has a much harder time, but she is always been so dramatic."

❧ Mom goes back and forth. She said it is hard, as it is new to her. True. However, she is also lying about some of it. She wrote a letter and addressed it Dearest "David" with quotation marks. She said that had no meaning and played ignorant. The only problem with that is she was an English teacher, and nobody addresses someone that way. The meaning was very clear, since I wanted to be addressed that way, she was only doing it to pacify me. That is not a good idea in any relationship.

❧ I am still early in transition, and my dad refers to me by birth name and gender. I am sure he'll come around, though.

❧ My mom, I believe, is in the middle and not sure of where I am on her spectrum.

❧ My parents were dead before I transitioned.

❧ I do not talk to them anymore; so I have no idea.

❧ Neither parent is alive. My sister, her daughter and children have no troubles with me. To the kids I am "Aunt Patty." Of course the kids never knew the *before* me.

❧ Only my mother lives, and she is 90. She does not get it, and refers to me as my birth gender.

❧ My parents passed before they knew the extent of my gender identity.

❧ Both of my parents are long dead, and I am totally convinced that neither would have ever accepted what I am. My grandfather on my mother's side committed suicide at age 33 and my grandmother always hated me because I reminded her of him. The secrecy surrounding his death eventually led me to believe that he was suffering from gender dysphoria.

❧ They are dead.

❧ My transition occurred long after both of my parents died. I believe my dad would be happy for me and support me. But my mother -- like everything else between us -- I would never, never hear the end of it.

❧ My mother has passed and my father is 74. He would not understand or accept my transition at all.

❧ My transitioning started after my mother's passing. Father is unknown.

❧ My birth sex. My mom is coming around, but my dad not so much.

❧ My dad and stepmom are wonderful about using my preferred name and pronouns. They introduce me to new people as their son (or stepson) and even get the little details like referring to my brother and me as brothers, not siblings. My mom, on the other hand, despite having known about my gender identity for longer, forgets more often. She calls me a girl, then rolls her eyes and corrects herself. But at least she does not try to stop me from transitioning. She tells me I have every right to do what I like with my body.

❖ Both passed away before my finding myself. My stepmom refers to me as the corrected identity, and she told me my father would have been fine with it if he had known.

❖ My family, if they talk to me, address me as the male that I was born. Never have they addressed me as who I am, Maya. All parents are different. See, being forty, my parents are old school. I do not think they will ever come around. That is why my family are my friends.

❖ My parents are deceased. My sister avoids pronouns, and we do not live near each other. My son calls me "My mom, he..."

❖ My family refers to me as a female. Because they love me and agree with my lifestyle. My grandma is not living anymore. Even though she treated me in a disrespectful manner, I forgave her, and I still love her.

❖ My father had passed away, but my mother was the only family member that never got my gender or name wrong. She wrote her own obituary before she died in 2008. She wrote she was survived by three daughters and our names and one son, my younger brother.

❖ Yes, I am 100 percent male to my mom. It is a great feeling. She always knew anyway; so it was fairly easy.

❖ They still call me by a male name. Even my mother did until the day she died. My Dad still uses the male pronoun to describe me.

❖ All my family members, besides my son, refer to me as

a female, which is my documented gender at birth. They believe since I was born a female that means I will always be a female.

❦   My folks both passed years ago. My younger brother still addresses me as my male self. He will never ever recognize a female. His wife, however, tries when she can

❦   They have not spoken or addressed me since I told them. They are just silent. I am a little afraid to see them in the next two weeks and how they will respond. I hope it goes ok.

❦   My mother still calls me by my birth name and ignores the fact that I am trans.

Chapter Sixteen

If you were religious before transitioning, how did you reconcile your transitioning within formal beliefs of your religion/church?

"I have not been much of a church-goer since I became a "Recovering Catholic," but about 15 years ago, a Unity minister explained that we do not get to choose God's challenges. We just get to choose whether to face them now or later. I chose 'now'."

⚜ I believe that god loves all his children: straight, gay, lesbian or transgender. I believe that god does not have a "sex" and created us the way we are to learn. This is, of course, in conflict with the traditional fundamentalist views of most churches; however, it is slowly changing. I believe that being trans is not against anything said in the Bible.

⚜ In my form of Protestantism, it is not an issue.

⚜ It has been hard more recently after a man who studied in seminary told me a story of a "man" who wanted to use the ladies room and refused to call her SHE, because, "It is complicated. HE has not had all the surgeries." Then he suddenly switched out of the blue to saying gays should never be preachers. He agreed when I said all have sinned and that all sin is equally sinful, but when I said, "If gay is a sin, do not pastors also sin?" he stuttered and said, "Um, pastors, uh, have PROBLEMS." Then he ran off to "help his wife clean up." I have not returned since he seems to feel superior and sinless.

⚜ I sought out trans friendly churches; still do. God created every one of us. Some with bad hearing, blind, or physical defects. He created both GAY, STRAIGHT and Dual-gendered individuals along with those born intersexed. It is up to us to find our strengths. While studying various religions, I joined a Unitarian Universalist church. I do not think I could attend a Presbyterian church, as they cannot associate with people of color or politics.

⚜ I have never been religious. I am a born again Christian in a relationship with God and Jesus. Reconciling was as easy as being born intersex, getting reading material, discussing it with other Christians, and using the Bible. It was easy for them to see I was born with a doctor making a [wrong] choice in who I would be.

⚜ I had been religious but questioning. Given the way religious people, like clergy, have reacted to me early in transition, I am now an atheist. What kind of God would ever make me like this and then allow others to treat me this way?

⚜ I felt I was not a mistake or wrong in my feelings but felt I would be condemned; so I left the so-called Christian church for a liberal religious group.

⚜ Prior to transitioning, I moved away from the strictness imposed as a child about attending church. I consider myself spiritual.

⚜ How about a 'spiritual' person? I 'saw' through religion at an early age. My challenge was that, from the perspective of 'enlightment', transsexualism along with everything else was a non-issue. However, that tends to ignore what we call real or what is experienced. In the world of non-duality, of course, that makes a type of sense. However, denying this existence right off puts you back in duality! In other words, one has to accept both -- this is just as 'real' as not real! Trust me; this is a topic for a whole volume of books! I am a female being on this plane of existence.

❧ I was raised in the Episcopalian church, and I do consider myself very religious. I have no conflict in my mind between my faith and my identity. God gives us bodies that He thinks we will like, but He is not offended if we change our minds. He might give a baby brown hair, for instance, and that person might go their whole lives dying it blonde because they like it more. We can do what feels right to us and get on with our lives as good, loving, and faithful people.

❧ My religious beliefs have never changed. I am a stronger believer and have always been since conversion in 1987. Prior to that, I did not believe. Now I CHANGE STRONG BELIEVERS WITH MY CONVICTIONS.

❧ I am a religious person, but through my years I was always told that I was going to Hell. I learned that we are all loved by the higher power. We all will stand for judgment.

❧ I am a Christian, and as a Christian, I feel I am still not in a positive light with God and Jesus Christ due to how I live my life as a female.

❧ Having been kicked out of the Catholic Church at 20 for how I felt and later being excommunicated by the LDS Church when I started transition, I have lost any feeling of religious belief. What I once held so dear to me was and still is used to condemn me as well as justification to discriminate against others and me. I feel it was my greatest loss of transition.

❧ I prayed. I now am more spiritual and believe in order to get good things, you must do good things; meditation helps.

❧ God loves me for me, and those who could not accept me for who I am are not true Christians.

Chapter Seventeen

Did you lose many friends during transitioning? Explain how you emotionally stabilized your life following their loss?

"When I look at the exodus of people who abandoned me when I announced my transition, I realized they were not my friends. Friends do not abandon friends. I have new friends who are friends that stayed with me during transition and after surgery."

✤ Knowing how most of my old friends have reacted, I have moved on and surrounded myself with more liberal and accepting friends.

✤ Yes, I lost virtually all of my professional associates and the friendship of my biker fraternity as well as the friendships I had with my ex-wives. I have now adopted my current spouse's friends as my own, although I am somewhat reclusive.

✤ Only my son. Others have quietly faded away - nothing significant. I did not consider those as 'friends', perhaps only acquaintances. Regarding my son, I spent time with my allies (notably my partner) and my therapist. I also get away up into the woods high up on the mountain here for solitude and collection.

✤ The positive path described above.

❧   Not many so far. I am not out back home to many, as I am at university out of state.

❧   I did not lose any friends because of my gender identity, but I did lose a good amount because I did not want to be treated badly by the people I choose to have in my life. I did not come out to my friends to be treated like dirt or to be the tail end of their jokes. For a long time, I shut everyone and everything out. I focused on building myself up and, when I was ready, I ventured out and made new friends, better friends.

❧   Being as I am somewhat of a loner, not too many.

❧   None, absolutely none. I think the transition is actually strengthening many of my friendships.

❧   I did not lose many friends during transition. I lost a few, and some distanced themselves a bit. For the most part, the people in my life were very positive and supportive. Even those that did not really "get it" were just happy that I was happy. Now that I am feeling more comfortable as the real me, they all realize how much more they like the new, happier me.

❧   Most friends either during or just after transition.

❧   Actually, I gained friends. When I left the US Air Force, I moved to California where I did not know a soul and left the old life behind.

❧   I believe I will lose some friends as the news comes out, but I have made many friends in the LGBT community to replace the ones that did not have the ability to see what I have always been.

❧   Here and there. Shrugging it off was easiest. If I am that easy to drop, then I do not need them.

❧   No I did not; those I lost were not true friends, anyhow.

❧   I lost a few friends through my journey in life. It hurt like hell. I figure, since I had no family, that my friends were family. But the ones that walked away made me stronger. They were never true friends, anyway. That made me alert about who I friended.

❧   I realized it was about them, not about me. I found new friends and 'family'.

❧   No, because it was I who walked away. I never really kept that many friends.

❧   I lost most all my friends. It took a while to feel that maybe they were not really friends. I feel what helped me was the friends I gained as who I truly was. I also have rekindled friendships with old classmates.

❧   Yes, but it showed me who really cared about me and who did not; so it was really a blessing.

❧   Just being myself truly

❧   I was pretty much a loner in life. I lost a few. I figured they were not my friends, anyway. The people who have stuck with me have been those I met in transition.

❧   They do not know yet.

❧   Well, I moved around a lot during my transition. Many have not seen me in years. I let them believe what they want. I am slowly coming out to many here on Facebook. So far, it has been a positive experience.

❧   A few of my hetero cis-male friends have stopped really speaking to me since I started transitioning. It is a bit depressing, but I know that it is most likely for the better. I do not want to be friends with someone who only wanted to speak to me because I was female. That is not a true friend in my book.

Chapter Eighteen

Are you the first person in your family to transition?

99.89% Yes

Proof:
You all are the
Pioneers

Publisher's Note: Many added the words, "As far as I know..."

Chapter Nineteen

Do you look up to anyone transitioning as role model?

"I do not look up to any one person specifically. I am inspired by how far the Trans community has come as a whole. There are now openly Trans athletes, models, actors/actresses, designers, singers, dancers, writers, producers, directors, and many more helping make a huge difference for the Trans community."

⚜ No. I do not have much to do with the trans or LGBT community. My circle of friends is cis women and one special man.

⚜ At my first support group meeting, I met the trans woman, Lisa, who became my best friend, was a mentor and a tremendous help during transition.

⚜ Jenny Boylan, Matt Kailey, Mara Kiesling: brave, tireless workers for change.

⚜ There are many I admire, but I cannot single out anyone.

⚜ I have had support from many members of ElderTG. [Ed. This is a newslist (listserv) associated with OnLinePolicy.net *<groups.onlinepolicy.net/index.fcgi/info/eldertg>*]

⚜ There are so many. From people I know personally here, members of ElderTG, books I have read, authors I know (e.g. Robyn and Emery Walters), people like Laverne Cox, and so many others that are out there on the public stage telling our story.

❧   I am following Mellanie Anne Philips' voice lessons. Stephie, someone on YouTube, helped me sort out feelings about being old and transgender. Genesis P-Orridge for presenting herself without trying to "pass."

❧   Several. My friends Sarina Reneigh, Shannon Lawrence and Ladys Victory (on YouTube), and many others. The reasons I see them as role models are their wit, personalities and their strength.

❧   My best friend's Aunt Megan. She showed me that I was not weird or that different growing up.

❧   I know a guy who was a cop and transitioned and who now is an interpreter. He always is smiling. First time we met, I assumed he was gay and cis-gendered and deaf because he was in an LGBT office for the deaf. Boy was I wrong! It sure shocked me when I told him I was transgendered and he said, "Me too!"

❧   Christine Jorgensen. I met her in 1970, interviewed her, and saw her again a couple of years later.

❧   I was alone for the better part of my life. I had no role model or mentor. I belong to a group now and have offered myself up to answer questions and to be there for those who need someone who has been through surgery.

❧   I would say it is the guy who came out publicly and whose story I saw in the San Diego newspaper some 35 years ago. The strength and purpose that he showed was an inspiration to me. Upon reading his story, I knew that this was right for me, and I never questioned my decision after that point. I can actually remember how I felt at that exact moment and my decision to have surgery, which I have never questioned.

❧   I certainly did when I was first coming out. It was very much in the way a boy looks up to men in that he hopes to resemble them someday. Now, I look up to those who advocate for transgender rights and who draw awareness to trans issues.

❧ No. I do not have much to do with the trans or any part of the LBGT community. My circle of friends is basically cis women and one special man.

❧ At my first support group meeting, I met the trans woman, Lisa, who became my best friend, was a mentor and a tremendous help during transition.

❧ Jenny Boylan, Matt Kailey, Mara Kiesling - brave, tireless workers for change

❧ I admire many, but I cannot single out anyone.

❧ I have had support from many members of ElderTG

❧ At my high school, there was a trans girl a grade older than me who was always very kind to me and open to talking when I needed it. She was not only a role model as a confident trans person, she was also one of my greatest supports.

❧ All those that suffer in transitioning are role models to me because they are going through the toughest part of their lives. They choose to continue to walk a path that could ultimately end up in death when hiding would be easier.

❧ My mentor and role model is Joan A. Sheppard. She has made me a better person, heart, and soul. I have learned from her that no one can make a life for you, that you will learn to make a life for yourself. She taught me how to see the good in people even if they are not so good. She really opened my eyes in life, and I love her for that.

❧ Just the really pretty ones.

❧ Christine Jorgensen. I went to see her movie, The Christine Jorgensen Story. I finally realized I was not nuts and I was not alone. I was a human, and I needed to find out why I was/am this way. I finally interviewed her in 1970 for a local radio station. In the PRIVATE interview, she outed me!

⚜   Tammy Matthew. She has been in transition for over three years.

⚜   Yes I do. I look up to Jimmye as a role model. She is extremely intelligent and wise. She has been through a lot with her transitioning and has taught me to be true to myself and grow tough skin since it is needed for survival.

⚜   I do not really have anyone I look up to on an individual basis. But I do look up to a lot of people who have gone before me. They empower me to know I am not alone and that it can be done.

⚜   No. I was my own role model. My therapist was annoyed, but that is how it was. It was time to listen to my own true self for a change.

⚜   Jamison Green and Jude Patton, while not role models for me as a male to female woman, are still worthy of my admiration as two who formed the early days of our community. I learned much from them and their experience, and that helped during my years as a transactivist/transadvocate.

⚜   Men I found on YouTube.

⚜   Honestly, it was friends I made online who got me out and into the community. It was [due to] their prodding that I am where I am today. Them and all those before me who showed me that there is life, a beautiful life, after transition.

⚜   Yes, seeing that there are other people like me made my transition go smoothly, I feel. His name is Beck, and he is helped me so much and [made me] realize I am not a box; I am human.

⚜   Alex in the movie XXY.

Chapter Twenty

The **Before**
and **After**
Photos

CommUnity In Transition

Chapter Twenty-One

Do you believe including transgender in the LGBT (Lesbian, Gay, Bisexual, and Transgender) acronym adds to or subtracts from the confusion?

"All four letters of the LGBT acronym have always been a part of our history and culture. The bravest pioneers of the Stonewall Revolution were transgender women. We deserve a place at the table and all deserve a voice. There should be no confusion in a common goal of equality for ALL of us."

⚜ I think it adds to the confusion. Transgender is about gender identity. Lesbian, gay, and bisexual are all about sexual preference. They are two mutually exclusive groups.

⚜ Sexual preference and gender identity are two different and non-related things. To be included in the group further confuses society; especially due to the fact they all assume gender identity and sexual preference are the same thing.

⚜ I think it is not good. HRC [Human Rights Campaign] takes credit for us but does not do anything to support us. People see drag queens and gays who are effeminate and say, well, transgender are one of them.

⚜   Sexuality and gender are completely different. Yes, we have things in common with LGB and working together makes sense. However, cis-normative individuals already have everything confused, and adding the T seems to just confirm their opinions and makes it more difficult for us T to explain who/what we are.

⚜   I personally feel that all genders should hold no ill to any other gender.

⚜   I think it adds to the confusion. Transgender is about gender identity. Lesbian, gay, and bisexual are all about sexual preference. They are two mutually exclusive groups.

⚜   I think it adds to confusion because LGB refer to defined sexuality whereas there is not necessarily a direct correlation between sexuality and transgenderism.

⚜   This appears to be two different questions. I have never had to deal with discrimination that I knew of. I seem to have been lucky enough to have been accepted both as being gay and as a male after transitioning. I think that having T added to the LGBT is a positive thing as far as promoting acceptance. But that said, I do not think that Gay people really accept trans people into the group.

⚜   I see two sides about the LGBT community. I am accepted in the women's community. Partly that is because Portland, OR, is a very accepting community. I do not identify very strongly with the gay male community. This city has all sorts of events that involve both sexes. Trans people are a minority of a minority. We need all the help we can get, and there is strength in numbers. On the other hand, the ignorant think we TS are all gay men.

⚜   T is a good part of queer (LGBT)

⚜   It confuses the issue. Many people get confused about effeminate gays and think that they are what constitute a TG.

⚜   I do not know enough about this topic.

✤	I believe the acronym LGBT should not include the T because it adds to people's confusion about transgendered people. Being transgendered is a gender identity issue and not a sexuality issue. I looked up company policies to find a job that had a nondiscrimination policy that included transgendered people. Thankfully, I did find a job that is happy to call me my preferred name and use the pronouns I prefer. Yes, it took a lot longer to find a job, but it was worth it to find a safe place.

✤	Since our history in the LGBT movement is one and the same, our fight to end discrimination and for equal rights under the law are the same, and the fact that many trans people are gay or lesbian, I think it is important that we are included in the mix. Others may feel differently. I have many friends throughout the community and have not experienced discrimination so far.

✤	I feel like those are two VERY different questions. Firstly, since the T is already a part of GLBT, I figure we should leave it there for now, even though I do not think it has done us much good.

✤	Subtracts. Because people see trans* as an orientation not an identity. I honestly believe that the T needs to be removed from LGBT.

✤	I think trans issues need to be much more included in the LGBT movement, and if people are "confused" by the T being included, that is a huge problem.

✤	The T should be removed. LGB in its meaning is about sexuality, and transgender is about gender identity. Within our own identity we also have our individual sexuality. L, G or B. Adding the T to LGB takes away our individual identity and lumps it as a sexual identity only. This causes confusion in mainstream society.

✤	No I do not. LGBT is for us all that are different. It brings lesbians, gays, bisexual, and transgender together. It is a group that you meet wonderful people in. It also shows us places where we all can go and feel comfortable for who we are. It is a group that brings joy and hope back into your life. It shows us bars, hotels, restaurants that we can go to and be ourselves. Plus, you meet great people that turn into great friends. I support LGBT.

✼ To me, adding anything other than a normal human term concerning gender will automatically be assumed as "odd" and relatable to outcast due to early humans' train of thought because those kind of people are still in the male and female generation. While we are in the male, female, LGBT etc. generation.

✼ I am one who believes in strength through numbers. This is where it adds. Discrimination against one is against any of the others. What is wrong is the divisions we have within ourselves. Yes, we have differences, but only in solidarity will we bring about change for the positive. Also, we truly have to be the T. We cannot sit by and expect the others to fight for our rights then condemn them when they do not. Far too many Trans identified people seem to sit back quietly or after transition just fade away into society.

✼ I feel it does. Now that I am seen as a straight male going into gay lesbian bars, I get weird looks. Funny how that works, but most of the guys I know stay hidden, and I do not get it, but after transition that is not the only thing defining us any more

✼ Oh it subtracts! Hey, I am not so much about having a same sex relation as I am with having body parts that agree with what my brain is telling me.

✼ I think that we all sort of deal with the same spirit of hate as the next person in that group. I feel we should all be together as one to help educate this world about these things, things that have been branded incorrectly. I do not think it adds confusion at all. It makes it stronger, another branch to what the world needs to know.

Chapter Twenty-Two

How do you successfully handle discrimination during the interviewing process while looking for employment?

"This is a hard one. While looking for employment, or even having an interview, you need to keep your head up and stand strong. This is called confidence. Never show weakness, as they feed on that. Your biggest fear may turn out to be the best decision you may ever take in your life. There is discrimination everywhere; it is the world we live in, but knowing who you are and having confidence within yourself, will show you that being different does not matter. Stay true to yourself."

⚜ I just applied for an internship in Congress with the most conservative member of that state. I used my new name, and they wanted me to start on Monday. I do not know what they would do if they did a background check and found female information on me. Time will tell!

⚜ I look in industries where trans people are. I try and point out my being a ready and willing worker, able to adapt or at least compromise in a situation. I am in business for myself, and I am in a specialized field. Many art people are considered eccentric anyway. I build architectural models, movie props, dollhouses, and museum enclosures for artifacts.

❧ Confidence. I have had zero issues with anything work related because of the transition. I have even switched jobs during my transition.

❧ This has not been a problem for me.

❧ I do not care what anyone says; there is no way to handle discrimination in an interview. You have to list your former name on background check documents prior to being interviewed. If you encounter a bad response, you go to another interview. No one can or will help you. You are the only person you can expect to help you. Get a job and try to move up.

❧ I get angry. Who would not? It is rather expected, and I am resigned to some. That does not happen anymore.

❧ I am retired.

❧ I am close to retirement and have not interviewed since I started transition. I have a lot of experience in my field. If that did not come across or if gender became an issue, I would walk out.

❧ I am not "out"; so it is not that much of an issue. I am discriminated against for not being masculine. I deal with that successfully by not being crushed when I am not hired.

❧ I am not out and still present as male; so I have not had to face it yet.

❧ I am fully retired and have no need to work and since my BFF (Ed: best friend forever) has hired me as her promoter and production manager, I have not experienced this part of transitioning. I know it is out there and feel for those in need of work who cannot get it due to society. Discrimination is not good in any form.

⚜   I would operate on a need-to-know basis, and if there were questions about my resume, I would tell them the facts.

⚜   Was not an issue for me.

⚜   As a transgender male to female if you are not passable, you will have a hard time getting jobs because employers are also human and see men as men and women as women. Some employers have a heart, and some do not. Some employers hire girls just to pleasure their ego or sexual appetite, and others consider girls as useful, productive team members. You just have to make the right choice in your choice of business, just like everyone else.

⚜   I worked for a very diverse company. My healthcare coverage took care of all my needs of transition.

⚜   I do not bring it up. I pass full time and do not have it brought up. But I had to quit other jobs when I first started because I hated myself for letting it [discrimination] happen since I could not prove it happened.

⚜   I have not found work being trans.

⚜   Move on and try to educate them that we are just humans.

Chapter Twenty-Three

How do you successfully handle discrimination by fellow workers during employment?

"This is simple. I have been there. You have to go to management and file a complaint. Never argue with a co-worker; they feed on that, and they see your weakness. You kill them with kindness; they do not know how to handle that. Most of the time they back off because they see no weakness."

❧ I usually remain silent on the issue.

❧ This was never a problem for me either when I was seen as gay or as a male. I never worked anywhere that anyone knew me as transitioning.

❧ I had to learn to speak up for myself and put my foot down. I am lucky enough to work in an environment where everyone I work with is very supportive. My identity is 100% respected and in no way affects my job or the way I am treated. When I have run into an issue with a coworker, I made sure not to take it overly personally, but stood my ground, went to management, and spoke up for myself. They listened and supported me completely and handled the situation, but not everyone is as lucky as I am to have such a supportive work environment.

❧ You ignore them. Whatever you do, no matter how

much you feel like crying, never let them see you weak. Weakness draws more attacks.

✤ I have never had to face that problem.

✤ I work for the state, and there are a number of strict rules and guidelines here -- and those have been expounded! In general, I tap into my ally network first, then I talk to management (very much on my side), and finally (never had to go this far) I would report it. There is a state office for gender relationships and they were instrumental in my coming out at work. As a result, everyone here knows I know them and have helped them develop their program.

✤ I am not out and still present as male; so I have not had to face it yet.

✤ I have no patience or tolerance for that at all. I do not "handle" it. I fix it.

✤ I stay quiet and let them criticize me until they are finished, or I let them do it in front of a manager.

✤ Now no one knows. I am a supporter for everyone.

✤ Since most of the work I do is done by myself in a small office, I have little interaction.

✤ I generally work by myself. I will dress accordingly if I know the client is transphobic.

✤ Years back, when I wanted to come out as Trans in 1970, I had to remain in the automotive repair business. It provided a cover. I went on transition when I became permanently disabled in life. I do my work on the side and most customers never actually meet me in person, anyway.

Publisher's Note: On almost every post for questions 23 and 24, "I have not had this problem yet."

Chapter Twenty-Four

How do you successfully handle discrimination by managers during employment?

"Managers hold power at work, but remember, discrimination is not tolerated in a <u>professional</u> business. Managers do have someone over them; so report it to corporate office. Discrimination in the work place is not tolerated, and corporate knows if they do not do anything about management harassment that we do have laws to protect us in the work place. But still, never show weakness."

Publisher's note: In 2014, most states and the Federal government still do not have laws that protect transgendered people from employment discrimination.

❧ You confront it, and you lose. You will never have enough of a leg to stand on to ever win. You start looking for a new job because you know you are going to need one.

❧ Again, I do not have this problem here. I am fortunate to work for government. There are very strict guidelines here, and management especially is held accountable.

❧ Overwhelm them with reason. I avoid being crushed and seek other employment.

❧ I am not out and still present as male; so I have not had

to face it yet.

❧ Go to their superior and use my higher intellect and level of sarcasm to my advantage.

❧ They do not know at my current job. Previous ones I just quit; since it was fast food, they did not care.

❧ I do my best to hold those thoughts in my head. I vent to others outside of the office. I am able to shrug a lot off these days. Here where I am, I expect to be treated badly.

Publisher's Note: On almost every post for questions 23 and 24, "I have not had this problem yet."

Chapter Twenty-Five

How do you successfully handle discrimination by customers, clients, patrons during employment?

"Professionally. If they were abusive to me, I would simply be icy cold to them in return. I am retired but when working, had jobs where there was little interaction with customers. Being insulting [in return] might feel good to me, but would hurt the business."

❁   I allow anyone to have their say. I am always truthful if I am found out or outed. At my age, I do not really care, anymore.

❁   What is funny is that customers rarely ever show hate or discrimination. The worst thing a customer has ever asked me is, "How far along are you in your thing?" It is a blatant question about the operation. I simply state," I am legally female," and leave it at that.

❁   I have witnessed 'hesitancy' on occasion; however, I am a very open and friendly woman, and once we get started, that usually goes away. I have feared this, but every time it was surmounted. Be open, friendly, honest, and outgoing.

❁   Avoid being crushed by the discrimination.

❁   I am not out and still present as male; so I have not had to face it yet.

✤   I will ignore what I feel is a deliberate comment the first time; after that, it is a free for all.

✤   I have never encountered any form of discrimination as I go out in mainstream society and promote the singer I work for. NONE, PERIOD.

✤   Discrimination by customers or clients: Remember you always have the right to refuse service to anyone who is disrespecting you in any way. It is your right, but still show no weakness.

✤   Was not an issue for me.

✤   I stay quiet and let them criticize me until they are finished, or I let them do it in front of a manager.

✤   I do customer service all day over the phone; so I just correct them and move on.

✤   Just being myself.

✤   Usually by staying silent on the matter. I just allow a dissention and try to get out as quickly as possible without comment.

Chapter Twenty-Six

When do you tell a new friend regarding your gender correction?

"It all depends. My opinion is that when someone starts to be a good friend, they should know. If someone is just interested in me -- well first, that is none of their business at this point. That being said, if the situation presents itself and this looks like a developing relationship, I will tell them. Certainly, I will tell anyone that I am in regular contact with: work, hair stylist, laser tech, electrolysis tech, etc."

⚜ As soon as I do not sense them as a threat. I tell people as soon as possible. If I can tell they are not angered easily, or they do not seem to be a physical person, I tell them right away. Otherwise, I feel like I am lying to them and hiding who I am. Why would I want to have people in my life I have to lie to? What kind of a life is that?

⚜ I only tell someone when I am at a point in the relationship that I am about to have sex with them. No one else needs to know.

⚜ *(I am uncomfortable with the phrase "gender correction" because it implies there was something wrong with us in the first place.)* I do not tell every stranger I walk past that I am trans, but if I meet someone new whom I know I will see regularly, I tell them right away. I am very open about my trans status, and if that is an issue for someone, I want to know it right away so that I can (a) try to educate, or (b) move along and not waste any time having someone in my life who has a problem with who I am. I will usually slip it into conversation nonchalantly and gauge their reaction from there.

⚜ Some know right away, and some do not have any idea right now. It is all a matter of who the person is and what kind of person they are.

⚜ Only when I am dressed decidedly female and addressed as my former "male-self" do I ever politely say anything.

⚜ I am open about it from the start. Everyone knows, and it really does not bother me. Despite hating who and what I was, it is all in the past and helped shape the person that I am today. There's nothing shameful about that, and there's no reason to hide it.

⚜ I do not unless they ask. Then I am honest with them if they do. I explain mind and body congruence

⚜ Has not yet happened on a wide scale. So far, I have tried to gain an understanding of that person's acceptance or otherwise of transgenderism before saying anything.

⚜ Being a trans advocate and very open about my past, it usually comes out sooner rather than later. In the early days, 16 years ago, my FTM husband and I used to speak of it as "educating the world one waitress at a time."

⚜ When the time seems right.

⚜ Within the first few discussions or interactions and before things get serious.

⚜ It has not happened.

⚜ I am not out and still present as male; so I have not had to face it yet.

⚜ Gently.

❀   Right up front. Boldly by saying, I was born a man, and if this bothers you, we need to now part company. The truth creates a strength that lies destroy.

❀   You always tell them from the beginning, because I have learned from doing so that you get a better outlook of who that person really is. It gives you better judgment on that person, which gives you the power to friend them or not. Always be honest to them but also to yourself.

❀   It varies with the person, my mood, my safety, and whether or not it matters. I may be the first TG person they meet, and it will open their eyes for the future. It might help someone else down the road.

❀   In the beginning.

❀   I do not. It is none of their business. Maybe after a few years, but it takes time. I do not want to put myself in a bad spot.

❀   If they ask, I will explain. If not, I am just being myself.

❀   I am very up front with everyone now. I am who I am, nothing more, nothing less. I deal with others on an as needed and need to know basis.

❀   The first time you meet them. I believe in being truthful with the people I am with.

❀   If it is a stranger, I do not unless I am spending more than a few minutes with them and never seeing them again. If it is a new person or a friend asking, I will correct them, just passing it in conversation. Like it is not a big deal.

Chapter Twenty-Seven

When do you tell someone interested in dating you of your gender correction?

- ➢ Depends on situation: Before dating-not long after asking out.
- ➢ ASAP, definitely before anything sexual happens.
- ➢ I do not date.
- ➢ Before sex.
- ➢ Someone interested in dating me would already know that I am trans.
- ➢ As soon as physical intimacy is going to take place.
- ➢ Within the first week.
- ➢ Before it gets serious.
- ➢ It has not happened.
- ➢ Generally, I am right up front about it.
- ➢ I am straightforward with people.
- ➢ Immediately.
- ➢ In the beginning.
- ➢ I married my partner.
- ➢ When feelings get involved.
- ➢ Trans lesbian; straight away.
- ➢ First date.

Chapter Twenty-Eight

What advice do you give to someone trying to have this dating conversation?

"Disclose your situation as soon as you feel that the relationship could be more than casual."

✤ Go for it; let it all out up front. Do not waste your time with someone who would not accept you when you could be building the beautiful life you deserve with someone who could not imagine their life without you. In my experience, if they are not open to going out on a first date with you after the conversation, they are not going to feel any differently about the third date after the conversation.

✤ Not dating yet.

✤ I do not advise others.

✤ I advise that you get to know the person as a person and only tell specific body info if you need to because the relationship has progressed to the point you are going to have sex.

✤ I am extremely open about my trans status. One look at my Facebook page will tell you that I am trans. So if someone is interested in dating me, they already know that I am transgender. I am afraid I do not have advice on bringing up the topic for the first time with someone you've already gotten to know.

✤ Be yourself.

✤ Well, this happened to me twice, once in a virtual world and once in the real world. There is a conundrum here: if you come out right away, it is a bit forward and presumptuous and perhaps a spoiler when they really do not know you well enough. If you come out later, then you were misleading them, concealing facts, etc. I believe there is something in the middle and being alert and conscious of the budding relationship should expose the proper time. Of course, there is always the downside.

⚜ Tell them up front; that way you know they like you for you.

⚜ Immediately. I am sure this is different for others, but I am up front about it.

⚜ I would rather be straightforward and lose them now rather than later. Just be yourself. You are beautiful and handsome in your own way.

⚜ Simply put, lies destroy a relationship faster than anything. To hide your past is to start a relationship on a lie. If they cannot handle it then, they will handle it less when they learn of the lie. I hid it from my fiancé and now we are no longer friends. She decided that the lie meant I lied about everything. I do not hide it anymore from anyone. I do not just boldly walk into a room and announce it, but if a relationship might pop up, I expose myself. But not to the general public.

⚜ As I said, always be up front with people, it gives better judgment on who that person really is. It tells you from the start if you want to talk with that person or not.

⚜ Be careful. Go slow. And be in a safe environment at the time.

⚜ First, you must find out if it is a safe person to tell or not.

⚜ To be open and honest.

⚜ I am dealing with this now. It is never an easy question,

but if there are feelings, slide it into conversation and then you'll know.

- Just treat me as a human being

- Be honest about yourself and others. If they wish to hate you over your being trans, that is THEIR problem, NOT yours. Remember , they cannot live your life; only YOU can! Listen to the Transperson describe their situation. I am not really all that female looking in the face anyway without makeup and hair styled. I work both ways anymore.

- Be open and truthful.

Chapter Twenty-Nine

Married with children (or not...). If you are already in a relationship before transitioning, when do you talk with your partner or children about gender identity and your transition?

"I found out on Facebook that my father was transgender. We talked to him about it. Now we talk about everything."

❧   Remain truthful; stand your ground if necessary.

❧   Day One.

❧   I talked to my daughter when she was eleven and kept her in the loop all the way through the surgery.

❧   I married a lady with children during my transition, and we did not tell her children of my previous gender. These children are now grown with children of their own, and we have no plans to ever tell them.

❧   I told her the day after I received my GID letter. I was asked to leave and did so.

❧   I lost my daughter in the divorce. It is the worst thing to happen since birth, and that is saying a lot.

❦ My spouse was well aware I had breasts. In time I told her about the hormone treatment I had had 18 years earlier and that I was on "T" to undo the effects. Over time, I told her more about my dysphoria. She encouraged me to be just me. I quit the "T" and a year later resumed the M2F hormones, making my spouse a part of it and explaining that if it made her unhappy or uncomfortable that I would quit. I considered her as an equal partner as we walked the winding road of transition.

❦ In my case, I kept up a constant dialog with my wife. I was not a cross-dresser, so this was all on a philosophical/internal level. The proverbial brown stuff hit the fan because of other issues, some of which were tied to this pre-transition phase. In general, I think one has to be as open as one can be with their spouse and hold the realization that this could be a deal breaker. Most important is to bring the spouse along with your own learning curve. They need to know everything you know and what you feel now. Ultimately, it is their choice for themselves. Some have a big issue with being "seen" as a lesbian. My partner overcame that, mostly by realizing society's labels are not real and are not based on fact. In her words, "I love the being that is you; that does not change." Regarding children: this depends greatly on age. If very young or if they are adults, then I would recommend you bring them along right from the start. For the very young, it will be nothing new. For the adults, they will gradually know as you know and will grow along with you. The harder issues are with the teenagers but also with adults that have had bad experiences or have issues (like my eldest son). If it is possible to scope this out first and if this situation is known, then a good therapist and research in the net groups and friends can help with suggestions. In my case, I live almost 5,000 miles away. I strongly believe that this had to be done in person, not a letter or email. It waited until my yearly trip back to the mainland. I firmly believed that it had to finish before anything became 'noticeable' in my transition -- in other words, I had to tell them before I started.

❦ This is simple. Honesty right away and in detail if the

CommUnity In Transition

conversation continues. Sit them down in private if possible. Their reaction can go in many directions, and a public venue is not the place to produce a reaction that might be embarrassing to them and shed a bad light on our community and your friends and family. Come right out and say it; do not beat around the bush. Then explain why, how, and what you are going to do and have gone through. To them, this is new, and they need to understand the truth, not a societal description of it.

⚜ This is a hard one. First, you need to be honest with your partner. Keep no secrets because, if you do, it makes it a lot harder. Tell your partner how you really feel in your heart. It does hurt you both, but being honest is always the key word. As far as children [are concerned], it all depends on their age. If they are young, it is hard to explain to them, and they would not understand [details]; so as they grow it is easier for them to accept who you are. Now, if they are older, it is harder because they do not understand. Be honest with them. Some will be okay with it, and some would not, but a child is easier adapting to changes than adults. Make sure your transition is what you want and who you are before messing up a family.

⚜ The most important thing is to never transition faster than your guardian angel can fly. That is, let your spouse/significant other have a hand on the throttle, not to say no but to let you progress at a speed they can absorb.

⚜ She was not surprised, as she felt I was gay. We remained friends until I began to find peace and happiness. I told my three children, and at first my two daughters were accepting but not quite fully understanding. I was there for my granddaughter's birth, my first, and the three of us saw each other a bit. My son really never got over the divorce. It was after the friendship with my ex ended that trouble began with my daughters. Today, the only connection is with one of my daughters. I have followed my therapist's advice and have given them space. It is been difficult, as I truly miss my children, but I manage, and as I see their successes in their lives know that in some way I was part of it. I also understand the suffering I caused by my twelve years of deep depression and self-hatred. I know that was so very hard on them, and as my own abuses of childhood affected me; it still does that to affect them.

✣ I am just me, the same person you fell in love with.

✣ First off, my partner was aware of my wanting to transition BEFORE we got married. Somehow, she got pregnant. She had three kids in a previous marriage. The father got the step kids in a custody battle after they were older. I was cross-dressing outside of the home. I searched out HRT even though I said I would not. I was soon removed [from HRT] because of a false positive blood test. I went back to being a Non Op. The now ex decided she did not wish to be married and took off out of the country with my son. I found another doctor and went back on HRT. She returned, as the son was slightly autistic, and she could not handle him herself. I was on HRT. She now lives with me and has been diagnosed with Lupus and severe Fibromyalgia. As friends, we all get along very well now.

✣ My now ex thought I was a Drag Queen BEFORE we were married. She knew about cross dressers and entertainers and was fine with them. My son saw me as an eccentric and sometimes strangely attired father. I had many talks with him early on, and I explained to him that there is a third gender. I am always truthful with him at all times, too.

✣ I have been married for eight years, together ten total. I have a seven-year-old daughter and a four-year-old son. I just started transitioning three weeks ago, and so far, for me, it is been wonderful. My husband is bisexual, and I am pansexual; so coming out has been much easier. As for dealing with it, my husband and I have random small conversations where we bring up issues and things we might have worries about and so on. I think being open and raw with your spouse is really the best course of action you can do. Share your fears, your worries, your likes and dislikes, goals. Do not shove it down their throat, but take the time out of the day to talk about it. Communication is a massive key in any relationship and must be put first and foremost. When I came out to my children, it was only a shock to my daughter. She was shocked, yes, but was keener on asking questions and was generally curious instead. I explain things to her every now and then and keep her updated on what is going on. If she has a question, I explain it to the best of my ability. Children are adaptive and always remember. They are not born to hate. Embrace them, include them, and never forget your love for them is the same as they feel towards you. Education is a big key to lots of things. Use this opportunity to share and educate them on acceptance and being open-minded.

Chapter Thirty

How do you address the public and management when using gender assigned public restrooms and public lockers open to everyone of the same sex?

"My birth certificate says female; end of conversation."

❧ In [Washington,] DC, it is law that you can use any bathroom you identify with without harassment. However, this week, a man at my school who works there blocked me after I entered the men's room as he was leaving to ask why I was in there. I know he had seen my birth name prior, but when I said, "WHAT?" He looked at me funny, said "Never mind," and walked out. There were only two stalls, the room was empty, he was not protecting anybody, and the women's room is down a different wing, so I reported him.

❧ Depends if I am dressed decidedly male or female as to which bathroom I use.

❧ I use the appropriate one. I am female, I was born with a penis; I use the women's rooms.

❧ I have no problems with assigned public restrooms or anything else. I have always looked feminine; so I still do.

❧ I use the public facilities appropriate for the gender I am presenting as at the time.

❧   Honestly, I have never had any issues using the restroom. I think everyone assumes this is a huge issue when it comes to understanding trans people and working toward trans equality, but trans people are using public restrooms all the time without even being noticed. Most people are not in the bathroom to noticing others.

❧   I use the bathroom matching the gender marker on ID.

❧   I have always been "passable" and never challenged. Just in case though, I carried with me a letter from my doctor explaining that I am transsexual and in the process of transition.

❧   Timing in when you attempt to do this for the first time is critical. I wore binders and stayed 'male' until about four months on HRT. This allowed me to grow out my hair; my body was able to transform enough, etc. Then I changed my name and gender, especially on my driver's license and Social Security card, threw away my binder, and came out totally as a woman. My first forays were always with my partner or an ally. At work, well the state has these regulations; use of the restroom according to your gender is one of them. My female allies talked with the other women in the building, and management talked to the hard-core.

❧   This is the thing I am most terrified of in public, but having my boyfriend, who is FTM, tell me I will be okay to use the restroom I want to helps me. If I am in an area where there are people who might be uncomfortable if I use the men's, I will use the women's for safety reasons.

❧   I am not out and still present as male; so I have not had to face it yet.

❧   I do not think about it. I just go and do it. At first, I used to have a friend stand by or sit in the stall until no one was present. Now, I just act like I belong, and no one pays attention. Normalcy breeds normalcy.

❀ First you check out your surroundings. Then go to management and let them know who you really are and find out if they accept you for who you are. If they do not, sometimes it is better to look for a facility that is acceptable for who you are. If you feel a little uncomfortable, sometimes it is better to go into the facility, do your thing, and leave. This way, you bring no attention to yourself. Remember, there will be that someone that wants to call you out. It just shows how uneducated they are about our lifestyle. Show no weakness.

❀ A cheerful "Yep, I am in the right room," is all I can manage. Then I leave.

❀ Has not been an issue for me.

❀ I do not ask permission to use the restroom. I just use the females' restroom, as any other female would.

❀ I really never had a problem with restrooms during transition. Never liked gyms; so that was not an issue. Today, after transition, I have never had any issues even in the gyms I now use.

❀ I just use the men's room. I do not change in public. I still have not had top done, but it is none of their business either. I do my thing and leave.

❀ I do not use a gym; that is out. As for restrooms, it depends upon my attire. If I dress as male, I will go use a stall in the men's room. When I dress predominantly female, I use a stall in the ladies room.

❀ I simply walk into the men's restroom and use the stall. No words needed.

❀ If I am dressed to look masculine, I will use the men's room. As a lady, I prefer to use a stall in the women's room or, when I can, the family restroom.

Chapter Thirty-One

How do successfully handle losing a partner unable to handle transitioning?

"Cry. Lean on your friends and allies. Realize that they have to follow their hearts and their issues. Also realize that it probably was a good thing; life could have been even worse given this situation if it continued. Feel happy and privileged for the love and time shared. Cry your heart out, wipe your eyes dry, and look back out to the beautiful world and to being your true self."

❧ You take care of you and remember someone will love you, and it will be better than what you had; it will be unconditional and what you've deserved all along.

❧ I am still working on that issue.

❧ Mine ended in divorce.

❧ You have to realize that living your life for yourself is the only way to be happy and fulfilled, and therefore the only way to find a happy and fulfilling relationship. I started coming out to those close to me, and when my partner at the time could not handle it, I went back in the closet for a long, miserable year. I eventually could not take it anymore; there was no denying myself. I wish to this day that I would stayed honest with myself, but it is amazing what fear of rejection can do. We are told all our lives we would be lucky to find someone to love us, but those who love us are just as lucky.

❧   You walk away. They are not going to support you in any way, and they will attempt to undermine it all the way through.

❧   This is not something I have had to face, as I was post-op before beginning to date as a woman.

❧   Mourn the bitch for a few months and then move on much happier as a human with a new, loving partner.

❧   Lost one. It was her choice, not mine. My life is more important.

❧   I see it as their loss if they cannot handle it and love you for you. They never loved you fully. Remember there is a love for everyone. You may not find it overnight, but you will find the love that is meant for you. It does hurt a lot, but you will move on. It is not the end of the world. It is just the end of someone holding you back.

❧   You go through the five steps of grieving. Then you are open to synchronicity. When you are able to live on your own without needing someone else to make you happy, then you are ready. Remember that when the student is ready, the teacher will appear. So it is with life partners/soul mates.

❧   There's always going to be more fish in the sea.

❧   It is not something I have dealt with. My partner could handle it, but I felt like I was a problem because I was so unhappy in my body.

❧   Remain friends and then move on.

❧   I do not know. I am still trying to come up with an answer.

Chapter Thirty-Two

If your partner made the transition with you, what were the complications?

"There's always complication. We talked; we try to see eye to eye. Communication is key to any relationship. It is not a matter of fixing them but showing them a different perspective."

❦ The complications have been finding viable employment paying enough to support myself. It is ongoing, and I am trying to fix it.

❦ I think with my partner it was self-image. She does not see herself as a lesbian nor would she ever be. For her, it came down to seeing this as social labels. She was heterosexual before and now she is lesbian -- but with the same person. Same love, same being, same relationship. That plus, I suppose, with being over sixty, there is a certain "I do not care what others think" aspect to this, as well.

❦ I have been there; it is very hard on them to be there for your transition. See, they stay around because they think they can handle the after-transition, but, really, they cannot. They love the old you and not the new you. In this case, it cannot be fixed. See, they do not understand that your looks have changed but not your heart. Your heart is what they fell in love with, not your looks, and some do not realize that the heart stays the same.

❦ It costs a lot of money to complete a full transition.

Chapter Thirty-Three

In the beginning, were you able to find a social network for strength?

"Net groups, email lists, web sites, and groups. Also, I started with a good therapist, and her connections allowed me to join support groups locally."

⚜ Hundreds on Facebook, including CommUnity in Transition. Many are state by state, with lots being local. Search and be willing to vacate the groups that turn out to be sex sites disguised as something decent. Check out the site before you post in it.

⚜ I lived in a college town and went to transgender support meetings at the university. As well, I had a very good support group online and later met many of those people in real life.

⚜ Originally, it was Transgendered Network International (TGNI), but it has pretty much dried up. For the past eight years or more, I have been a staff member/administrator at Susan's Place <www.susans.org>.

⚜ I have used only one network for assistance. This is the ElderTG newslist of about 100 members.

⚜ Net groups, email lists, web sites and groups. Also, I started with a good therapist, and her connections allowed me to join support groups locally. Also, my network of allies, which included management and people in the state office of gender relationship. So building a network of allies and connections [was easy]. There was one woman at work who was an antagonist in just about everything. She attempted to sway other women at work into denying me restroom privileges. My network found out about this and reported it to management. They went up to the state gender relationships department and out to Lambda Legal. By the time I came into work, legal notices plus state policies regarding restroom usage were posted on all bulletin boards and this woman was summoned to the front office! (She was told that I have a right to use the woman's bathroom, but that management would see to it she would be comfortable; they offered to place a port-a-potty in the parking lot for her!)

❖   I used online Empty Closets, under pseudonym Deaf Not Blind. I stopped because there was unlimited bigotry against all Christians who were struggling with identity issues, even though they were not preaching at anyone. Atheists were hateful to us all! It really was shocking that the non-profit was allowing this, until I found out the guy is a pornographer and had been in trouble for another site getting boys to be in his pornos. He blocked me when I announced I was leaving, as some admins are not trustworthy and kept me from removing my posts, pix, and telling my friends there how to contact me. I think the group is good, if they remove the two men who started it. They need to be under investigation for abuse, and I fear our words were giving them ideas for new porn.

❖   I chatted with others for a while on tgchatroom.com. There they comforted and supported me, as well as encouraged me to ask questions to those who had transitioned long before me. My relationship with the people on the site ended because I moved to a place where I no longer had Internet connection.

❖   My first contacts were support groups; I still use them for strength.

❖   I had no social network for support.

❖   I found an on line chat room that let me realize that there were others like me. I now use trans* sites as well as Facebook.

❖   At the time I transitioned, in the late 70s, there was no support system to speak of. We knew there were other guys but my doctor discouraged us from talking to each other. I did talk to a few people briefly, but we did not have the social media available today. I never had any problem using the men's room. I find men are much more private about using the men's room than women are with their restroom.

❀ YouTube was a lifesaver for me in the beginning. Many trans men were documenting their transitions -- the social, emotional, and physical aspects -- and it not only made me feel less alone, it prepared me for what was ahead and gave me hope, something to look forward to. I also found people there I could turn to for advice or just for a word of encouragement. It would have been much more difficult and confusing to start my transition without the help of social networking.

❀ I am in a handful of "FTM" Facebook groups, but more often than not, I do not find anyone in there that I can truly relate to.

❀ No, but I also have not really looked.

❀ I used the internet to find someone I could learn. I found a local cross-dressing group that met in St. Pete. My fiancé and I went to a few meetings and invited some of them to our place for a party. Then we went to the Christmas get together. We dressed up as you would for a ball. But upon arriving, we were being put in a back room that was used for storage. Chairs stacked up, carpets filthy, and it smelled. We walked out, and I was in tears. It was at this time I realized they were all just going from one closet to another. Hiding from mainstream society. On top of that it, was an LGBT facility, and they were hiding us. I left and never went back. I decided then and there I had been hiding for 40 plus years, and I was not anymore. We ended up going to a regular Mexican restaurant for dinner and were treated wonderfully. I have never looked back, and I have done nothing but grow on my own since.

❀ Social Network never worked for me. What helped me were my true friends and the family I created. I am not saying the

Social Network does not help; it just did not for me. Yes, I am on Facebook, but sometimes it is not cut out to be what we want it to be, though I learned the "Tgirl Friends" is a wonderful group of girls that are just looking for friendship. Some will question you. It is only to help them deal with and understand the transition. They also become great friends.

❧ Yes, it is called "This is H.O.W." aka The Regina House in Phoenix, Arizona.

❧ I discovered a community in which to immerse myself. I later formed a support group with a friend but was soon asked to leave and was banned. My crime? I was too political and openly out. I was speaking where and when I could, and it was not looked upon kindly. I found another and kind of stayed around even after transition. After a while I found I did not need any support but was there to give support. But as time passed, it was as if I was just there; so I keep connected but have begun to move on. Today, I continue to be an activist and advocate for the LGBTQ with a focus on Trans needs and issues. I find my greatest comfort working with LGBTQ youth, as I see a better tomorrow in their eyes. They are our leaders of tomorrow.

❧ I found groups in Facebook and my local area. We are all different. I do not want to hang out just because we have one thing in common, so I stepped away. It was filled with drama. I hate drama.

❧ Back in the sixties through the eighties , there was no network, just gay bars, and I have always detested them. When a support group was formed in the late eighties I was not able to go. It was in an area where too many knew me. I came out to a co worker. I went to her and more or less practiced being a girl. In the early nineties, the group was still going, albeit weaker. I found my strength in a Northern Virginia group. There, I felt like I had gotten a college scholarship in transgender studies. I went out in public my first time to that meeting and because of their warm welcome, I was able to go to bars dressed and soon to a church dressed and from there it seems like

I went everywhere dressed.

✤   Too many to chose from.

✤   I relied on TGEA [Transgender Education Association, Inc. <www/tgea.net>], a support group in Northern Virginia. I kind of went to college as I met people there who were extremely well versed on gender reassignment

✤   I have been working online for over four years now as a freelance artist, and 100% of my clients have been wonderful. I came out on my business site, and everyone has been fantastic. A lot of them are my support. My online friends are also supportive, and I use Facebook to keep my family updated on all things going on. I like to use LiveJournal <www.livejournal.com> for looking at discussions about FtM and Facebook groups to ask and communicate with local FtM groups. It really brightens my day chatting with these wonderful people with whom we can share our fears and joys.

✤   Social networks are full of pitfalls like TERF [Trans-Exclusionary Radical Feminist] trolls. I deleted most of my social network sites early in transition.

✤   Pre-military (before the age of 17) I had none. During my service, I made a few connections, mostly through Virginia Prince. Later, I found a transgender Bulletin Board Service (BBS) in San Francisco before the Internet [World Wide Web] existed,. From that BBS, I found connections to support groups. Then the Air Force sent me to Greece for a year. I separated June 30, 1985 and drove west. There I found a link to a support group. And, as they say, the rest is history.

✤   Right now, I only have membership in a mailing list. I am planning to go to a weekly support group.

✤   I use Facebook and have had no problems with this.

Chapter Thirty-Four

Be greater than your label.

122 people responded to the questions of sexual orientation and gender identity.

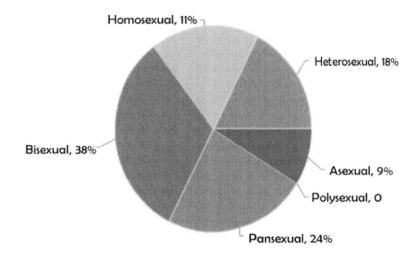

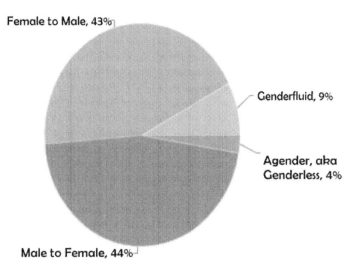

Chapter Thirty-Five

Which legal network do you use for assistance?

"My partner and I formed the Coalition for Transgender Rights in Virginia after working with the DC Trans Coalition. We try to keep as up to date on changing laws within both the state and the nation. I have used the Transgender Law Center, The National Center for Transgender Equality, and other national organizations. As a Navy veteran, I also keep abreast of veteran services."

❀ I got a good one recently at Whitman Walker Clinic [Washington, DC]. Volunteer legal assistance there will help you in many ways, and streamline the name change and gender process.

❀ I have not had to yet, but I am looking into it just in case. We have a transfriendly lawyer in Missouri.

❀ There is no network here in Virginia, and I dare say there never will be. I am in Virginia and there is not any network of any kind for us. [Editor's Note: See other Virginia citations in this chapter.]

❀ I remained in the same state while transitioning and since I pass as a female while transitioning, I have had no difficulties

❀ When I transitioned, it was extremely easy in the state I lived to change my driver's license and even my social security info.

Only this past year did it become possible for me to change my birth certificate gender; I am in the process of doing so, but this had never been a problem for me until recently.

⚜ The law can never overcome my legal gender marker. My ID identifies me as female, and regardless of the law, I am a girl. They cannot legally change my gender marker for their purposes.

⚜ Advice from other transsexuals guided me through the legal stuff such as changing my driver's license. I DID have a problem with one individual in the San Francisco passport office. My therapist used her connections to solve the problem.

⚜ I am in Canada, and most provinces treat transgender persons equally with all others.

⚜ I use Lambda Legal, Susan's Place, Laura's Playground, and a number of other web groups. I am also plugged into a number of resources where I keep up to date on what is going on.

⚜ Not so far.

⚜ I have never had a need to use one.

⚜ I do not use a legal network, I do not need anyone telling me that my lifestyle is wrong, I heard this my whole life. Like I said, the ones that give you strength are your good friends and the family you have created. Legal network, lol; the laws are not the same from state to state, and I will not listen to people telling me that what I am is wrong. Their politics in disputes are not my cup of tea. [Editor's Note: The legal networks to which we refer are those that help transgendered people.]

Chapter Thirty-Six

How did you pick your name, and have you corrected legal documents?

"I changed both my given and surname. I chose my given name from one that was given me in China (where I worked for a while). It was a feminine name. I picked my surname because of where I live and its meaning."

❦   My name was one I picked long ago, and I have not made any legal changes yet.

❦   Although my name "Donnie" is not legal yet, it is similar to what my birth name was. For some reason, I have always liked the name "Donnie." I did not want to pick a name like many other FTMs do where their name is "Jason" but they spell it "Giayzionne." [I wanted] something relatively normal without calling attention to itself.

❦   No, I have not gotten my name or gender marker changed. I picked my name because I wanted to keep my initials for my parents' sake. I picked Kyler-Eli because Kyler Elijah did not sound right and I wanted the Eli part. Leon is what my mom picked.

❦   In the process now. Should all be done by May [2014].

❦   My mom was going to name me David if born a boy; so I took my rightful name. My state identification card expired this year; so when I flew home, I got to get a new one with my correct name and gender. Because of the legal help free to me in DC, I hope to have my name and gender fixed by June [2014].

❦ I picked my name over 15 years ago. I cannot remember the reason for the first name but the middle was chosen because my mother once told me it is what she would have given me if I were born female. I should have all proper documents changed within the next three to six months.

❦ I wanted a name that was feminine and not masculine related. My gender status was changed by a letter from the operating surgeon sent to the state I was born in, and now I have an amended birth certificate saying I was born female.

❦ My femme name was taken with respect for a person I admire for her great social work and understanding.

❦ I was lucky enough to have a gender-neutral name; thus, I did not change my name. I did change the spelling of my first name slightly. I only needed a letter from my doctor to change my gender marker on my driver's license. See above for birth certificate. I changed my driver's license and Social Security as soon as I got my letter. I only recently was able to correct my birth certificate.

❦ I picked my name by starting with the first letter of my birth name and flipping through baby name books to find names I liked that rang well. I would imagine myself answering to them and see how they felt. Once I narrowed the list down, I looked at the meanings behind each name and landed on the one that fit my personality best.

❦ Yes. That was in Washington State, early in my transition. It was an easy process that required a letter from one's gender counselor.

❦ I picked my name when I was thirteen years old. I filed for legal name change pro se with the court and published it. The state of Nevada has a Department of Motor Vehicles (DMV) form to change legally your gender, and all you need is a doctor's sign-off. All easy, but costly at $365.00, including publication of the name change. One doctor's visit and poof, a real driver's license, the first real one ever. Social Security was easy, also. I was unfortunately born in Wyoming. My birth certificate change will require the SRS (sex reassignment surgery) operation. I am planning to confront it head on to attempt to make the case that if they are going to require surgery, they should pay for it. I do not have time now and do not really need it anyway.

❧   It was the first name that came to mind, and no other has seemed to fit. I began changing my documents shortly before going full time. The California DMV treated me with respect. I told the clerk I needed to change my driver's license. She escorted me to a manager who was quite helpful. With my carry letter, I walked out with a shiny new driver's license with an "F" in the right place. All my documentation was changed in 1986/87. I had no significant problems except for the passport, which was deliberately held up by one man in the passport office. Not the office, just one individual.

❧   I went by the meaning and found something compatible with my twin daughters' names.

❧   I changed both my given and surname. I chose my given name from one that was given me in China (where I worked for a while). It was a feminine name. I picked my surname because of where I live and its meaning. As I stated above, I wore binders, etc. until about four months on HRT at which point I came out fully and started my real life experience (RLE). I had coordinated this with coming out at work at an all hands meeting where people from legal and the gender relationship department came to speak about current policies. I had worked with them to include trans*. At the same time, I changed my name, then driver's license then Social Security, and then name on my birth certificate (gender will be changed after SRS). I am waiting on passport now. I had my doctors and therapist write letters and sign documents that allowed my gender marker to be changed within this state. The only issues were timing between the different changes; in other words, it was all the red tape.

❧ Yes, my driver's license is the correct gender. I did it after legal/medical transition. My name change was done in court with no problems. My name is gender neutral, and I said I liked it better. My name came to me in a dream, believe it or not, just as someone had told me it would.

❧ Yes I did, but you have to change your name through the courts. As for your name, the name you choose is the name you will have for the rest of your life. Your name is not given to you; you choose the name that fits you deep down. I made my legal change in my second year in transition. I changed my first name to Maya but kept my middle name spelled differently for my last name, which is Shayne.

❧ Yes. I am still working on my birth certificate. I am very busy, and when I am not, I am very tired.

❧ I am currently in the process of a marker change in Virginia.

❧ I corrected my license when I was able to. My name was easy, as it was something I was always called as child. Then it was meant to tease but to me confirmed whom I knew I was. Middle name, after my great aunt who understood me as a child. Changed all my documentation, birth certificate. diplomas....everything after surgery. I even corrected my military records.

❧ I have changed my name, but I am still working on the gender. I picked my name with the help of my mom. She asked me to keep Ash, so I did, but my middle name is now Xavier. I have always felt like one. I know you need surgery in Kansas to amend your birth certificate, but in Missouri you do not; so that is why I am calling the attorney.

Chapter Thirty-Seven

In the beginning, were you able to turn to your religion for strength?

"I am spiritual but not religious and was lucky to belong to an accepting and thinking congregation. I did see a minister, and she was a lesbian."

⚜ I have not found much use to the online queer religious sites. I am sure they help some people, but it just felt like a farce, that some want to change the Bible to suit their needs. I have no proof that their interpretation is correct. I do know one thing stands out in the Bible: God is love. Jesus gave the command to love one another, everyone. His example was hanging out and befriending thieves, liars, prostitutes, and he told a woman living with a man unmarried who was worshiping God wrong (like a cult would today, perhaps) to bring her "husband" to see him. Something tells me the "Christians" who tell LGBTQ they are living in sin and should change or not come to church and cannot be pastors/priests are not like Christ, but are in fact Pharisees. Jesus did not mock and attack the "sinners"; he did attack the Pharisees, however! This helps me hang on, knowing if I am unwelcomed at all by the people in suits, I am most welcome inside the Pearly Gates. That is what counts.

⚜ Again, nix religion (defined as an organization), but I am spiritual. There are many others of my persuasion, and I relied on this network to help both myself and others to understand this within this spiritual context.

⚜ The Bible is a constant source of strength; however' organized religion can be problematic. I try to attend LGBT friendly churches at this time.

❧   I believe but do not attend a Church. I am a KJ and DJ and a local church has hired me for DJ work on occasion. They are very open and know about my past. In fact, I was a preacher for a short time. My decision to leave was not based on my desire to be a woman. It was in 1987 that I left the ministry and for an entirely different reason. However, my knowledge of the Bible has helped me to show those who use the Bible to condemn me how to change their thinking.

❧   I am a Christian. I have no religious networks of strength.

❧   God made us all; that includes gays and transgender people. I first attended an MCC church. They said they want transpeople. Talk is cheap. I was raised Presbyterian with a small dose of Hebrew. Today, I am a member of a local Unitarian Universalist church. I found that attending a Unitarian Universalist church has done more for me than anything. I can say I have real friends there.

Chapter Thirty-Eight

What is your medicine regimen since the start of transitioning: What personal benefits, risks, and harms have you observed?

Publisher's note. The following narratives are not endorsed by the publisher or editor. No hormone or hormone blocker regimen should be undertaken without having a medical doctor's prescription and care.

⚜ I am on 0.5% T gel, daily. I am unusual in that it works strongly on me; most people need a full dose of 1% or injections to transition. I have not had any bad side effects after six months.

⚜ Spironolactone , Finasteride, and Estradiol.

⚜ 4 mg Estradiol daily. I moved up to this dose gradually from 0.5 mg. 100 mg Spironolactone since day one. I had some severe abdominal cramping for the first two weeks but nothing major since.

⚜ The consistent prescription would be testosterone, which I have been taking since I was 29. I have always been physically active but have never followed a regular exercise program. I am considering it now that I am over six foot five. The benefit of the hormones is the physical changes expected. I have had few adverse effects from the hormones other than some sleeping problems, which have started in the last two to three years.

❧ The only thing I take is testosterone. I watch what I eat and make sure I am getting enough vitamins and nutrients in my diet. So far, I have gotten a perfect bill of health, and testosterone has not changed that.

❧ Two hundred mg spironolactone oral daily divided am/P.M.. Eight mg estradiol sublingual divided a.m./P.M.; 5 mg finasteride in the am, sublingual. Ten mg per day of Prevaria taken only the last ten days of every month, sublingual.

❧ Premarin. Initially 2.5 mg, then 1.25 mg post surgery. Others: a couple of antidepressants, vitamins, over the counter meds, as required.

❧ Vitamins A, B, C, D, glucosamine, and baby aspirin Prescriptions: Trazodone, Nexium, Crestor, and Estrace - six mg daily.

❧ I am under the care of an endocrinologist and following his guidance. Everyone is different. I am on Spiro and Divigel (estrogen) plus over the counter progesterone. My general practitioner has me on vitamin D3. The expected physical changes occurred (breast growth, redistribution of fatty tissue, facial changes, hair pattern changes, more emotional, cry more, etc.). My breasts were sore for about six months as they grew. They are small, but that is expected. Pretty much everything I had read from others' experiences and from what the doctor described has happened. No real surprises except that I do still have a libido. (From what I read, that seems to be 50/50: some do, some do not.)

❧ I stopped taking estrogen tablets and started injecting testosterone cypionate, all by prescription of course. I am moodier, happier, stronger physically, and, oddly enough, do not talk as much.

❧ I began transition with 100 mg spironolactone and 2.5 mg Premarim per day. I dropped the spiro after surgery. Now, at age 77, I take only 1 mg Estradiol every other day to keep the hot flashes and night sweats at bay. I have liver enzymes checked annually. I do cardio and pump iron 3 mornings a week.

❧ Vitamins, hormones and exercise/weight lifting. I also stopped drinking as much as previously to give my liver a break.

❧ Fenugreek, 3 times a day, Soy Iso-flavones 3 times a day. 2 MG of estradiol once a day. Very strong feminization, facial changes, skin changes, softening of hair and slowing of hair growth. Very good breast growth and testosterone levels below that of a normal male. I have experienced no ill effects with this regimen, mental or otherwise. Some mood changes and upon keeping a record of the times I found it is consistent with a P.M.S schedule like a GG [genetic girl].

❧ I have taken Premarin for years, along with spironolactone. Now I inject 1 ml every two weeks of Estradiol Valerate along with the rest. My turn out has changed dramatically. My skin is soft, and my breasts and hips have formed the way that they should. I have yet to have any work done to my body.

❧ I take Estradiol and spironolactone. I see no changes.

❧ HRT under medical supervision and after surgery still do. I felt good. It was as if a poison was removed and replaced with perfection.

❧ I just take my shot weekly; nothing else really changed other than I got stronger.

❧ Spriolactone , Estradiol, and Finasteride. I first noticed my depression going away very rapidly. I had been on Depakote for years. I no longer was on this drug, as the doctor was made aware by my moods being way more even. He took me off and told the endocrinologist to just allow me to have female hormone therapy.

❧ Using hormones.

❧ I get my first shot of testosterone starting at 200 mg every four weeks.

Chapter Thirty-Nine

Do you regret transitioning?

"I have never regretted transitioning. This was a matter of life or death for me. I had to transition in order to live as my true self."

❀   I have not regretted it so far. I enjoy not being called miss, and [enjoy] being called sir, and my voice not making them apologize and "correct" to miss. I see myself in mirror now, not a boy in drag with womanly shapes. Dysphoria is about gone, depression is gone. My issues are changing to homework and school deadlines as all cis students struggle with, too. I do not have to act now, nor try to please everyone by dressing in a way that makes them happy for me and makes me feel awkward and immoral. (Yes, dressing like a beautiful lady with curls and makeup felt like acting on stage and immoral to make men think I was a female.) I will question my decision every so often, thinking if it is a good idea or should I quit now. My reassessment has always been so far so good; going back would be intolerable. I love who I am now. I can speak my mind and am not weird; I am "normal."

❀   Not for a second.

❀   I do not regret transitioning.

❀   I do not and have never regretted transitioning. I still know it was, and is, the correct thing for me to have done. Although wishing the surgery had been more advanced when I did it, I do not regret having the complete surgery done when I did it.

❀   I regret the way society treats me so well to my face, but refuses to allow me the respect to look past my gender presentation and see my life skills. I also regret it every time a medical professional suggests I move to San Francisco.

⚜   I have never regretted transition. Not even for a moment. No worries except initially when passing was an issue. That is ancient history.

⚜   No, I am so happy to finally be me with a body and mind in congruency.

⚜   It took me years of analyzing my life, critically trying to disprove that I was transsexual. I had guidance from a number of therapists over this period or phase. There were a lot of layers to peel back. I have heard this many times - the more you push back against your femininity the harder and fiercer it becomes. I had to make sure that I was not "making this up," that I "wanted" this, instead of this being the real thing. The break-through came a bit more than a year ago; it was a light switch. I am now so firm and resolute; this is me. After nine months on HRT and six months RLE, I am so happy and so free -- I am now able to be myself -- no putting on facades, no pretending, no misinterpretations of my body language, etc. I have not regretted one moment of my transition.

⚜   My goodness NO! It has been my saving grace! My depression, GONE!

⚜   No, never. I do not regret becoming my true self, even if others have a problem with it.

⚜   Best thing I ever did for myself. I have to believe that all will be tended to. Being true to myself helps me be more compassionate of what others are going through.

⚜   No regrets whatsoever.

⚜   No regrets. I started hormones 18 years ago because in my heart I was a woman trapped in a man's body. To start transition you have to be mentally ready for it. Challenges will come at you from all directions. Only you can make your transition what you want it to be. Never do what someone says. What works for them may not work for you. Look up transgender and be educated before you take any big steps.

❧ I do not regret anything about transitioning except how long I waited to do it.

❧ No!

❧ I do regret it, but I still do it because I am mentally a female even if dressed as a boy. I am still considered odd and treated worse as a boy than as I am as a passable girl.

❧ No, I do not regret it one bit. I would be dead if I did not. Some days I feel like I will never save enough for top surgery, but I know in time it will happen, I stay humble; I give back to youth in schools. When I do worry or get scared, I look in the mirror and am amazed at the man I can finally see.

❧ In reality, I have actually never been happier. I have never for a moment regretted anything. The only thing I would say I even regret is that I did not do it sooner. I do feel though that having a career with a very diverse company and one [that is] fully understanding and accepting helped me succeed in transitioning. I work with LGBTQ youth, and I impress the importance of education because it is a huge benefit when it comes to successful transition.

Chapter Forty

Discuss positive conversations you would share with someone who is politely confused on "transgendered people."

"I tell people who are confused that Trans people are the same as them. They have hopes, dreams, families, lives, jobs, and a lot of them have marriages and children, too. I tell them that there are many variations and experiences of being Trans. Some people feel that the gender they are on the inside does not match what people see on the outside and take steps to change that. Others are fine with being one or many genders on the inside and do not bother to make any changes at all. I tell them all of these choices are both valid and respectable. If people ask me why I "chose" to transition, I tell them that I did what feels best for me. I tell them that it was not so much a choice as a calling to express my authentic self. If asked why I transitioned knowing people might cause me harm, I tell them that I feel uncomfortable living a lie. I want to express who I

am; I do not want to hide behind a facade any more than they do. I also tell them that by denying who I am, I am hindering my personal growth."

❧   I explain that cross-dressers like to visit the other gender but that transsexuals want to BE the other gender. As to a matter of "choice." I explain that the choice is whether or not to pull the trigger.

❧   I am mentally a female even if dressed as a boy. I am still considered odd and treated worse as a boy then as I am as a passable girl.

❧   Simply said, it was never a choice; it is who and what I am. A decision made was one of survival. In the past, I would explain, but today in workshops, I just ask, "What do you see?" Sometimes, I run across one who just does not understand, and I ask, "Are you comfortable in who you are gender-wise?" When they reply that they are, I ask, "How would you feel waking up one morning and looking in the mirror at a body of the opposite gender?" They always say they would not, but I say that is something I dealt with for many long years. As for causing hurt and harm to others, I say, that I have, especially my children, but I also hurt someone else, myself. I know that I so hated who and what I was pretending to be that it was slowly killing me.

❧   I explain it is not a choice. You just have to educate people and, if it is not going anywhere, walk away. That person should not take away anything from you. As long as you are happy, that is all that should matter.

❧   I was a cross-dresser or doing drag all my childhood and young adult life! LOL The fact is, my body just looked odd in a dress no matter how hard I tried. I thought when I put on all male clothing, not just one piece, I would feel weird, but actually when I looked in the mirror the drag queen was gone! Yeah, I saw the real me, not in drag; I was normal now. You got it backwards. So far, nobody has done me harm, and I am not scared because God is with me. There is nothing to fear but fear itself; it can kill you. I had to transition. I wanted this since I was a child! If I had known when I was ten about hormone blockers and transitioning, I would have asked my grandma to help me. I know it is hard for you to grasp, but that is good! I am so happy you are not like me. It is very confusing to be a child knowing something is wrong, and being afraid to tell anyone because they may think you are evil. Nobody wants to be trans; some just are. If you are scared others may harm me, pray for my safety.

⚜   I tell people who are confused that Trans people are the same as them. They have hopes, dreams, families, lives, jobs, and a lot of them have marriages and children, too. I tell them that there are many variations and experiences of being Trans. Some people feel that the gender they are on the inside does not match what people see on the outside and take steps to change that. Others are fine with being one or many genders on the inside and do not bother to make any changes at all. I tell them all of these choices are both valid and respectable. If people ask me why I "chose" to transition, I tell them that I did what feels best for me. I tell them that it was not so much a choice as a calling to express my authentic self. If asked why I transitioned knowing people might cause me harm, I tell them that I feel uncomfortable living a lie. I want to express who I am; I do not want to hide behind a facade any more than they do. I also tell them that by denying who I am, I am hindering my personal growth.

⚜   I like being able to share social secrets with my trans brothers.

⚜   People will judge you for the rest of your life no matter what you do. You may as well do what makes you happy if you are going to be judged regardless.

⚜   I try to explain that being transgendered is no more a choice than choosing the color of one's eyes. It is only presentation that could even remotely be considered any sort of choice, though for some trans* people, even that is not a choice but a destiny.

✼	I often answer these kinds of questions. Most people mean well, and do not mean to be ignorant, but are simply uneducated. I have no problem being the one to educate. I simply remain calm and explain in the best way that I can that my gender is not a choice any more than a cisgender person.

✼	I explain how it is not a lifestyle or a choice. I will usually ask them what color their eyes are. I then ask them how much input they had in making their eyes that color. That is what being born in the wrong body is. It usually drives the point home. If it does not, I explain to them how I threw up every time I looked at myself in the mirror for seven years preceding transition. I will tell them that I wish I could devise a pill that would make others feel as I did prior to transition for just 1 day. I tell them if they could all feel it, they would never question and never hate again.

✼	Being transgendered has nothing to do with sexuality. It is all about being of one gender and having a body that is in conflict; i.e., that of another gender.

✼	In coming out, I have these conversations all the time. The important aspect is "politely confused." First, gender and sexuality are completely independent. Just as many transsexuals are hetero, gay, lesbian, bi as cis-normative people -- same percentages (only reverse the concept of hetero and gay). Second, we are this way from birth. I talk about brain similarities but also mention the body map; those that lost a limb can still tell you where their fingers are. This area is in the same location in the brain. But I go on to say that this map (for me at least) also describes internal plus external aspects of my body. That is one reason why I know that my penis does not belong there - it is NOT in my body map. This all goes to say that this is NOT a choice. Gender is akin to hair color or eye color; it is just one more aspect of being human. The difference between cross-dresser and transsexual to me is that, dressing is normal -- there is not 'pleasure' in dressing -- this is average/everyday how I am supposed to be.

❦   I would attempt to explain how gender role is distinct from physical gender and the ideals of feminine and masculine. I would say that I am transitioning because it feels like a more comfortable position to be in while dealing with confusion about gender roles.

❦   I tend to only talk to people about this in a safe place. I generally do not tell anyone about my condition unless they ask directly.

❦   It is a response of doing what is true to me. I dress for the occasion I am in, not who I am. No use climbing on the roof to fix a leak with a face and heels on.

❦   I moved into a 55 plus community apartment complex; so I had the questions thrown at me tenfold. I sat with several over coffee in the beginning (almost three years ago). I started with the reason going back as far as I could remember. Then explained how it is something that happens prior to the birth in the womb: the how and the why. Then I just be myself. Not ashamed of who I am. I find that once people are aware that it is truly not a choice, they understand, and then, over the course of friendship, they learn more. I have been here almost three years now and am one of the most loved people in the building. There are all walks of life living here, and they have taught me how to deal with people of different walks and educations. My life has never been so full since I have had to learn more about myself through others.

❦   If someone asked me why do I choose my lifestyle. I tell them that I did not choose this life; I was born this way. I also tell them that this is not playing dress up; this is a lifestyle that people are born this way. I also tell them that if they have any questions, to feel free to ask me anything. And I will be open and honest to what transgender is all about. The more questions they ask, the more they learn on this lifestyle. I am an open book with no shame on who I am. I am a role model, an educator to anyone who does not understand what a transgender person really is. We are all human, and we all have one life. So make the best out of your life as you can. Life is too short; so always be honest and true.

❦   I have only really had a few people who did not know too much about FtM or transitions, and it was my delight to educate them on any questions they had, personal or not. I found it ten times easier to quench people's curiosity rather than blurt random things in their face. I do not tell if they do not ask, but I am an open book if they do. I will say that I was, of course, born in the wrong body, as I feel I was. I have held it in for many, many years to myself. And so on. I have gotten great feedback. Some confused still, but nothing harmful. I usually get the comments, "Well I am fully supportive of you!" and those make my day.

Chapter Forty-One

What are the top books you would suggest for those transitioning?

"I would suggest reading everything available. The more one knows, the better when making an informed decision about what if any surgery to have done. I would also suggest searching out and reading every website you can find as well as joining any email lists both for information and support. Again, being as educated as possible is the better way. Social media has been a great advancement in finding support for those who want to transition."

❧ Some things he [Jamison Green?] worded in a way that was perfect, and I had not had words to express. It explains about his transitioning, starting of the FTM support groups, how MTFs had more visibility, actions of lesbians towards FTMs who come out, and relationships with other cis men.

❧ I just did tons of research on the internet about it. I never read a book because I find most things about trans folk are the point of view of the writer only. I know how I feel and what I am. I researched technical things.

A list of the most recommended books:

Becoming a Visible Man
by Jamison Green
ISBN-13: 978-0826514578

True Selves: Understanding Transsexualism--For Families, Friends, Coworkers, and Helping Professionals
by Mildred L. Brown
ISBN-13: 978-0787967024

Whipping Girl: A Transsexual Woman on Sexism and the Scapegoating of Femininity
by Julia Serano
ISBN-13: 978-1580051545

Transgender Guidebook
by Anne L Boedecker
ISBN-13: 978-1461006206

She is Not the Man I Married My Life with a Transgender Husband
by Helen Boyd
ISBN-13: 978-1580051934

Transgender Complete
by Joanne Borden
Kindle Only

Crossing - A Memoir
by Dierdre McCloskey
ISBN-13: 978-0226556697

Transgender 101: A Simple Guide to a Complex Issue
by Nicholas M Teich
ISBN-13: 978-0231157131

The Bible.

I am Jay
by Cris Beam
ISBN-13: 978-0316053600

Beautiful Music for Ugly Children
by Kirstin Cronn-Mills
ISBN-13: 978-0738732510

DRAG411's Official Drag Handbook
Created By Todd Kachinski Kottmeier & Steve Hammond
ISBN-13: 978-1312021037

Publisher's Note: Thank you for mentioning 2011's The Drag Handbook, the largest LGBT compilation book in drag history until the following two books took the title in late 2014. Drag is another subject I have little knowledge of, but I opened my company to print. Every copy of the revised DRAG411 Handbook benefits The Joshua Tree Feeding Program, a nonprofit, all volunteer charity feeding entire families struggling with HIV/AIDS every Wednesday for over twenty-five years.JTFP.org

DRAG KING GUIDE
"So you want to be a Male Impersonator"
ISBN-13: 978-1-312443204
Created By Todd Kachinski Kottmeier

DRAG QUEEN GUIDE
"So you want to be a Female Impersonator"
ISBN-13: 978-1-312-443228
Created By Todd Kachinski Kottmeier

She is Not There: A Life in Two Genders
by Jennifer Finney Broylan
ISBN-13: 978-0385346979

Transgender Warriors :
Making History from Joan of Arc to Dennis Rodman
By Leslie Feinberg
ISBN-13: 978-0807079416

Chapter Forty-Two

Did you legally change you name to match your correct gender?

"I changed my legal name in court in Washington State. I changed my birth certificate and passport after surgery to reflect name and gender marker change."

❧ I have not changed my name.

❧ In the process.

❧ Made the legal change about six months into HRT, and it never really caused any issues. I do not ever look back, not even for a moment.

❧ I did recently get a court order to change the spelling of my name and will shortly be changing this on my birth certificate as well as the gender marker since it can now be changed where I was born. It has only taken 37 years for me to be able to make this change.

❧ My name is legally changed as well as my gender marker. I have no idea how my family feels because it has been 19 months since I have spoken to them.

❧ Of course. I changed every document as soon as possible after going full time. Court ordered name change.

❧ Yes, I legally changed my name about two years before I had GRS (gender reassignment surgery). This was all part of my RLE. My family accepted this, and my daughters provided strong encouragement.

❧ I planned this to coincide with the start of my RLE, at which point I changed all my documents to reflect my new name and my gender. Because I also changed my surname, some in my family felt I was abandoning them. However, I had been using my given name as an alias for quite a long time.

❧ Yes. Family unsure of their reaction, even though they have been notified.

❧ I made my legal change in 2006. Does my family know? The answer is no, because my family walked away from me. So I feel that their not loving me gives them no right to know the real me. They are stuck on the boy, but that boy died years ago. I do not need to prove myself to them or anyone. All I depend on are my friends and my made up family, and most of all to be true to myself.

❧ After surgery. Has had no effect as far as I know.

❧ Yes, about a year in so I could find a job not in fast food. They already called me Ashten other than my grandma and uncle; they switched to Ash.

❧ I am currently doing it this year. My will already reflects the male to female last wishes.

❧ I changed my name legally a year ago. Changing my name was difficult on my family. Since they are so used to calling me my birth name, they often slip.

Chapter Forty-Three

Have you had surgery to align your anatomy to match your correct gender?

"I had 'top surgery', also known as bilateral mastectomy with chest reconstruction, which I was very happy with and which was legally required for transitioning. I went to Portland, OR, one year after starting hormone therapy. The best parts were looking like what I felt I was, being rid of the 'evidence' to a great degree, and having people see me as who I am, a male. I was 'fully conscious' and self-aware all the time, instead of a rare peek before it was safe to be me. The negatives are that I cannot sing anymore from my voice changing, losing my hair (yes I am vain), and not having a male life to look back on."

❦ Yes. Dr. Toby Meltzer performed SRS on my sixty-third birthday in June 2000. The decision was made after being detained by security guards at a U.S. submarine base commissary following an employee's complaint that I had used the ladies' room. I was immediately released, the commissary manager apologized, and I never saw that employee again. The surgery cost $22,000 back then, including the follow-on labiaplasty and a tracheal shave to remove the telltale Adam's apple. Breast augmentation two years later cost another $5,000. Electrolysis cost another $20,000 because I was a tough case.

❧ I have not completed my transition yet. It costs a lot of money to complete a full transition.

❧ I did. I made the decision in 2003 and had it performed in 2008. It was covered by my employee health plan. It was performed in Trinidad, CO, by Dr. Marci Bowers. Positive aspects? Happy, peacefully within myself and the world around me. Negative? I guess being treated as second class because I am now seen as a woman.

❧ Yes, I have had hysterectomy covered by insurance, as there was a family condition of pcos cyst endometriosis; so I found a doctor willing to help. Three positive things: no more pain for one; two, no cancer worries; three, I can change my gender. Three negatives: I will never have bio kids, taking time off from work, and my family realizing this is who I am. I know I can adopt or ask my brother to help when I am ready. Low income, and yes, I got a second job to save money.

❧ I am pre op.

❧ I have not had surgery.

❧ Not yet, but I intend to as soon as I am financially able.

❧ I have had complete reassignment surgery. I started the surgery process when I was thirty in 1976 and finished within three years. Actually, my health insurance covered my surgeries, but I do not remember what the cost was at that time.

❧ I would love to get facial surgery to help me to blend more, but I know that I will never have the funds available to complete surgery; so I do not pine over it. It is what it is, and it must be accepted. I am a woman regardless of what I have in my panties anyways. I have complete control over who sees what is in them. I do wish I could do work on my face, though.

⚜ SRS on December 5, 1987. Once I found that I could have a life as a woman, there was nothing that could have held me back. I had an appointment with Dr. Biber, but 31 days before my surgery date, he broke his arm. I went to Dr. Seghers in Brussels Belgium. It was $3500 plus airfare and hotel. About $5000 total. That choice of surgeon was a mistake, as my vagina was only about two inches depth with no inner labia. I developed a fistula. I have never been functional down there in spite of two reconstruction surgeries. Between all that and having had testicular cancer, at this point my abdomen is a mass of scar tissue. At sixty-seven, I do not expect to have sex with a man, anyway. Maybe in my next incarnation. But hey! At least I no longer have "the lump."

⚜ Yes, I had my surgery on July 1, 2013. I went to Dr. Brassard in Montreal, Canada. The cost, including travel, accommodations and taking my spouse, amounted to $23,000. The affects were all positive; however, the recovery time took the whole summer; so I suppose that is one negative aspect. Another is having to deal with the bureaucracy in getting my gender changed on my birth certificate and passport. Low-income people are supported by grants from the Province of British Columbia but only after undergoing stringent screening by psychologists and psychiatrists.

⚜ I am in the process of scheduling my affirmation surgery. I am hoping to have it within three months from now. I have done a lot of research, read day by day diaries from my friends, and talked with a number of people that have gone through SRS.

⚜ No surgeries yet, I am still doing my research before I take any steps. I want this to be right with no regrets for what procedure I choose.

Chapter Forty-Four

If you had the operation, what were the greatest risks of the operation, regret, and recovery?

"No regrets at all. The pain was manageable, and everything went great and beyond my expectations. I do not need additional corrections."

⚜ Positive aspects were having my physical body be gender correct. Not having to use a binder or "pack." Negative aspects would be not being fully functional sexually, not really being able to go without a shirt in public even after surgery, and not being able to urinate standing. There were no options for low-income people to have surgery at that time as far as I know. The greatest risk was from infection, which could result in complete failure or various degrees of failure of the surgeries. Dr. Laub was my surgeon, and, yes, he explained everything and prepared me for the surgery outcome. There was pain, but it was worth the results. After time, I do not foresee doing any other procedure. I do wish I had done surgery that would have allowed me to stand to urinate. I foresee the surgery results producing more and more functional results. One other drawback I have experienced was having the testicle implants showing up on CT scans. While no one has said anything or questioned this with me, it is something to be aware of. My only regret would be in the results not being more cosmetically correct. I did go back to have more corrections to my chest surgery that were mostly cosmetic. The results are very good and may be even better today.

⚜ SRS December 5, 1987. My choice of surgeon (Dr.

Seghers in Belgium) was a mistake as my vagina was only about two inches depth with no inner labia. I developed a fistula. I have never been functional down there in spite of two reconstruction surgeries. Between all that and having had testicular cancer at this point my abdomen is a mass of scar tissue

⚜   Still in process.

⚜   My chest reconstruction left some obvious scarring, but I am older and nobody cares by our age. We all have scars here and there. There was very little pain.

⚜   Pain was minimal, but I was one of the few with nonstandard nerve location and ended up nonorgasmic. Very rare but, at my age, never a big problem.

⚜   I have not had the operation yet.

⚜   I was so high in happiness, I never truly felt pain. Regrets, none, other than that I did not do it sooner. Changes for the future: that all insurance plans cover it and that surgeons be made to accept health plans when patients have them. My surgeon was the only surgeon in the US that would work with my health plan. Every other surgeon required payment up front with a promise of help in getting reimbursed. One even said that I was lucky to have a health plan that covered it. I replied that I was on disability and on a fixed income so where was I to find the fee. Her response if there was a will there was a way. That is the problem, most [plans] did not cover it, and when they do, doctors do not accept it. Also, my plan paid nearly twice the cash price so the doctors fear that they would not get paid their fee was incorrect.

⚜   Hysto is just part one; top for me is next. I feel it will be more life changing, as I am very top heavy. The hysto was fine, all laparoscopic with nice recovery.

Chapter Forty-Five

Many of this book's audience will be people sitting quietly in their homes, terrified to be alone, searching for an overall scope of transitioning. What would you say to these people to bring them comfort?

"Transition is not easy. It is not cheap or without loss, but if done with research and support, it can bring happiness never attainable without it. Being someone who is not authentic but a vision of what others define for themselves is not life, but a hidden spirit of a person always trying to escape, always hating as they appear. Escaping that mold others have defined is becoming true in who you truly are. As your true self, there is no stopping who you truly are."

❧ Hey guess what? You were not the only one! Yup, I thought I was too. It is good to know there are words, such as dysphoria, to explain how we feel and that we can finally talk about it with someone who really does understand is not it? At the same time, it sure is sad there are so many of us, thousands, spanning every nation of the globe. There are too many hurting people, all these children, and many are children of God who think if they tell anyone ever they will be shunned, hated, kicked out of groups, and lose those they really need and love. God does not want us to live a fake life, and wear a mask, does he? So we have a problem here, my brothers and sisters, one of ignorance and rejection. Not everyone has taken Biology 101 and knows that not all those with XX come out as women, and not all XY are really men. Now it is either up to us to inform them or to go stealth like the others and to let more little tykes suffer as we did. Want to try to be the hero and change things with me? Let's begin.

⚜   I would suggest a therapist experienced in our issues. Then I would ask them to think transition through, thoroughly. I tell them not to [transition] unless there is no choice. I would tell them that transition was the hardest thing I have ever done, emotionally, and that it was no piece of cake, physically. It is an expensive way to go. I tell them to keep their sense of humor. It is a great help when dealing with the ignorant and stupid and it is a real help when the people do or say really stupid things.

⚜   You will find your place. There are kind people who want to know you, who want you to be happy and healthy, and who want to watch you succeed.

⚜   Never ever let go of ambition, your dreams, and your goals.

⚜   Please, follow your hearts. There is nothing wrong with being the person that you want to be. Believe in yourself. Some people will make it hard on you, but they are the ones with the issues, not you. I am very proud of my dad for the life he has chosen. He is happy and healthier than ever before. Find your inner self and let it shine.

⚜   No matter what you do with your life, make sure that you are doing it for you and nobody else. Nobody else can tell you what to do to be happy; only you can decide that. I wish you the best of luck with whatever choices you make.

❀ My main comment would be to tell them that they do not have to face life as a transgender person alone. There are support, assistance, love, and understanding available.

❀ Face the future knowing this will be a change that makes you right with yourself. That is the most important part of the whole experience. This is what makes going through all the phases and jumping through all the hoops worthwhile. You are not alone, and a friendly shoulder is as close as your computer or phone. Much has changed since the early days, and there is much more support available today. There is never a wrong question to ask. Be strong, be sure, and never look back.

❀ Transition is not an easy road by any means. It will show you a deep strength you never knew you had. No matter if you are transgender or not, being your true and honest self is the most important thing in the world. You can and will be loved for exactly who you are.

❀ There are people out there like me who want to do nothing more than to help you.

❀ IF transition is right for you, stand up, take a deep breath, and get to it. Over the years, I have known literally hundreds of trans people. Of that number, I have only met two who regretted transition. Both had serious unrelated mental issues. But follow the Standards of Care. Do NOT try to do it on your own. Hormones are very dangerous things. Used properly they will do wonders. Misused, they can kill you.

❀ You are not a freak, and you are not alone. Do not try to do too much at once. Take baby steps. Do not get frustrated dealing with the bureaucracy or with uninformed individuals. Rejoice in every positive step you take. Be proud of you and most of all, try and stay happy.

❀ Hi. We are in this together; you are not alone. Each day,

the world is progressing in our favor. There is a long way to go, but we have already come so far. It seems the hardest thing to know is if this is real and exactly what is this; why am I like this? Know that there are lots of us out here -- kindred spirits. Reach out, find us, find your allies, create your network, then use them; lean on us, let us help you. There are so many self-doubts, so much hidden and so many layers that need to be expunged. You need expert advice. Find a good therapist, and once you are sure he/she is "good," then do not hold back; be truthful, honest and sincere to yourself and to your therapist. So many people I know of that were afraid of what he/she would think and held back, only to delay their happiness, their true-ness. Aloha and big hugzzzz, Sifan

❦ All is vanity.

❦ I would say, you are not alone. Talk to someone, join a Facebook group, or even look for support groups that meet once a month in your community. If you look around, you might be shocked by the support you see. There is always someone willing to listen and help; so do not be afraid to ask.

❦ Be true to yourself. Do so without fear and do so with love and compassion in your heart.

❦ JUST BE YOURSELF and know that I, Kyler-Eli Leon, love you for you.

❦ Never underestimate the benefits of playing dress up. Really, just get a box of mixed clothes, and put them on and jump around. Put on boy clothes, girl clothes, androgynous clothes, and make up outfits for genders that no one has even tried being before. It is amazing what you discover about yourself when you behave like a kid again. You are beautiful, and every single one of those outfits will look stylish as hell on you. Let yourself relax and be as completely silly as possible. You will feel better.

❦ In our lifetimes, we are dealt many blows. Some we cause ourselves by our actions; others we have no say in the matter. As a Transgender you had no say in the matter; it is what you do with that gift of experiencing both sides and walks of life that will define your future, your happiness, and your successes and failures. Grasp this part of your walk in this world and do it proudly and without question. Do not push yourself upon those that do not wish to hear it. Just calmly walk away, knowing that you planted a seed. That seed may germinate and grow, or it may wither and die. It is not your fault if it dies. Know that you will face many trials and tribulations along the way, but each one will make you stronger if you do not allow it to destroy you or pull you backwards. You are going to find out at journey's end that you were able to experience a life few get to experience. You are a true explorer, and you can leave your footprint on humanity for the greater good.

⚜   This is your life; do not ever do something you do not want to because most work cannot be changed. So if you do not understand how the procedure is done, please look everything up on your computer and get educated before you take that big step. Like I said, some procedures can NOT be changed. And stay true to yourself.

⚜   You know who you are. Believe in yourself.

⚜   Remember that you are Number One. Although you must consider other people, this is about making YOUR life better.

⚜   Humans will always be humans. So let them be humans and let yourself be yourself. If you believe in God and Jesus, then we will all be judged in the end. If you do not, then do as you will.

⚜   You are not alone; do not ever feel you are. There are billions of people in this world, and if one does not accept you five others will; just stay positive, and life will show you the way.

⚜   Be realistic as you age [about] your ability to find work, to be the opposite gender in the real world. Too many have a "Pollyanna" view and will not plan forward. Do not allow yourself to be boxed in, either. If you want it bad enough, you will devise a plan. JUST BE REALISTIC!

❧ Just be yourself and do not rush your transition. Take the time to do it right and work on your transition.

❧ You are not alone. Everyone has to start somewhere in their transitioning journey. Be true to yourself and do what truly makes you happy. Only you as a person have to live with yourself. Respect yourself, and others will start respecting you. There are so many transgendered people out there and resources to help you with journey. A good place to start is a documentary called Trans Generation along with Facebook groups and support groups. We as people all have a journey to go through. You are loved and not alone.

❧ Be realistic as to expectations when you are transitioning. Consider your age and make allowances, as older transgender people are not going to have the skin, genitalia growth, and physical changes a younger person will.

❧ You are not alone. You are not the first, and you will not be the last. When you are ready to [transition], We will be there with open arms waiting. We will be there to help guide you, lend you a hand, and help you along your way. Do not ever forget. You are not alone.

Perhaps the most helpful thought expressed:

You are not alone,
You Are
Not Alone!

Current Zinnia Press Books

ZinniaPress.com, infamoustodd.com, and 14,000 retailers

"Two Days Past Dead"

*It is hard to be the good guy when you succeed so well being bad.
This is the Auggie Summer's dilemma. The story, based loosely on the
tales of Todd Kachinski Kottmeier, follow the precocious child as he torments
Holly, Michigan with his wild antics. One of his ventures, selling candy in 9th grade
catches not only the press but also amusement of the drug cartel early in its' own
infancy. Auggie Summers finds himself in the forefront of one of the most dangerous
organizations on Earth, trying to remain the silly, mid-western boy from the small
town of Holly. The tale follows Auggie, as he becomes a man trying to find
redemption from the people harmed in the tales created during his life.*
By Todd Kachinski Kottmeier with Steve Hammond

"Best Said Dead"

*A New Year's Resolution for the rest of your life.
Those brief minutes after a person dies should be so funny.
Many religions and beliefs define different paths for each of us. Rarely do we
discuss those precious moments between death and the final destination. This
hilarious comedy opens the possibilities that for a moment, a person vanishes
into the memories in their mind*
By Todd Kachinski Kottmeier with Steve Hammond

"Following Wynter"

*What happens when you get married only to discover your partner is secretly a
famous female impersonator? Hilarious comedy play. Ethan discovers his newlywed
husband is the flamboyant drag queen Wynter Storm in this whimsical farce with an
important message of believing in yourself and your friends... even if your friend is
Serena Silver. This play is staged around the world to benefit local charities.*
By Steve Hammond and Todd Kachinski Kottmeier

"Alone In A Crowded Room"

*Fifty Steps To Self-Worth. A Game Plan.
What if ten thoughts out of fifty brought you to the place you wish to be in life?*
By Todd Kachinski Kottmeier with Steve Hammond

"Joey Brooks, The Show Must Go On"

A humorous, real story of The First Lady of Ybor from the days of El Goya to present day. Female Impersonator, Show director, hostess, author..."Old school, new school, no school... who gives a shit? I'm too old to go to school. I barely remember last week. When I get too old to remember what the fuck I did when I was young ...ger, I'll just open of these books and laugh my ass off. I wonder how many other queens had this much fun becoming one of the icons of their community. Too funny. I just called myself an icon. Hell, I must be a queen. Only a female impersonator could call themselves a diva, a queen, a star without people giggling behind her back. Giggling is good. A twenty-dollar bill is better.

By Joey Brooks and Todd Kachinski Kottmeier

"CommUnity in Transition"

Compilation conversation with the world's transgender readers
We sent over a thousand invitations to the transgender community
around the world asking them to share wisdom, advice, and compassion
for those questioning or struggling. No restraints, using topics they created, as they guided the conversation over forty chapters and fifty topics. By the close, these remarkable people created the largest compilation book in transgender history. They opened their heart with these words

Created By Todd Kachinski Kottmeier with Dr. Robyn Walters and Emery C. Walters

"Turn Around Bright Eyes"

VERY VIOLENT Few crimes in gay and lesbian history rocked a nation as great as The Drag Queen Killer. The country seemed paralyzed from the first ring of the chain tapping on the concrete as they pulled Cassandra to her death, until the very last brutal killing. The murderous rampage seemed buried in the media suffering from a barrage of tales from the 9-11 terrorist attacks.

By Steve Hammond and Todd Kachinski Kottmeier

"Waiting On God"

A simple recollection of two old men waiting for their turn to talk to God.
A Two-Act Play.
By Steve Hammond and Todd Kachinski Kottmeier

"The Official Drag Handbook"

We sent out 2,700 invitations; these messages they sent back.
The first internationally successful compilation book by impersonators.
Created By Todd Kachinski Kottmeier

"DRAG Stories"

True tales from drag performers across the nation. Tales sent by Candi
Samples , Demonica da Bomb, Vivika D'Angelo, Chastity Rose, Naomi
Wynters with Alexis Mateo, Dmentia Divinyl, Lucie Bruce, Wendy Kennedy,
Miss GiGi, Chance Wise, Rico W. Taylor, Rachel Boheme , Bob Taylor, Stefon
Royce Iman, Daisha Monet, Patricia Grand, Shook ByNature, Esme
Rodriguez , Lady Guy Eunyce Raye, Charley Marie Coutora, Jezzie Bell,
Tiffani Middlesexx, Angel glamar, Anson Reign, Jayden St. James, Ma'Nu
Da Original, Rachelle Ann Summers, Champagne T. Bordeaux , Gilda
Golden, and the humorous craziness of creating the original DRAG project,
"The Official Drag Handbook."DRAG Stories is the first forum published by
the drag community for the drag community.
Created By Todd Kachinski Kottmeier

"DRAG Parents"

Performers look to drag mothers, fathers, friends, and fans for insight,
compassion, and guidance as mentors. This book honors those special people.
Over 140 entertainers contributed wisdom and words for this historical book,
making it the largest project of its nature in LGBT history. Drag Parents is
the first published book on male and female mentors
Created By Todd Kachinski Kottmeier

Drag World vol. I and vol. II

Drag World started as the largest drag magazine in the world, but focus
transferred into collecting the wisdom to create books for the benefit of the
HIV/AIDS community. This is the two largest editions.
Created By Todd Kachinski Kottmeier

Crown Me!
Nation's top crown holders share wisdom on winning competitions.
Hundreds of invitations sent to the titleholders, pageant promoters, judges,
and talent show hosts to share their insight on not only winning pageants and
contests but also owning the stage every time they perform. Their topics
included auxiliary steps to success needed for song selection, dancing,
movement on stage, props, backup dancers, creating your own edge, personal
interviews, steps to success for winning the talent category every time you
step on stage, on stage questions, evening wear, and creative costuming. They
discussed in their own unedited words, wardrobe changes, makeup, hair,
shoes, when is the time to compete, qualities needed for a judge, and the top
misconceptions of contestants competing in the pageantry systems.
Created By Todd Kachinski Kottmeier

"Why Me, Harvey Milk?"
"It is hard to fight for equality when you see someone less looking back in the
mirror." The Harvey Milk Festival asked a simple writer to be their first
Master of Ceremonies (Emcee). The writer struggled understanding his own
value to accept such an honor. In those struggles, he realized his own
insecurities are shared many other people. The following year, his second
speech for the festival challenged people to be active in the world, far beyond
the LIKE button on a social network. This book challenges two years of
attendees to change the world by renovating their own place in the world.
Contributing writers added supplemental resources.
By Steve Hammond, John Behr, Emily Burton, and Todd Kachinski Kottmeier

The Forum
Directory for the Male and Female Impersonators.
Created By Todd Kachinski Kottmeier

Opie and the Story of Forest Heights
A children's story of friendships and morals.
A Childhood tale of Willow, a small child that runs away into the
forest to hide from sadness. Willow is found by three small chipmunks
that teach her the adult lessons of learning to be happy
By Todd Kachinski Kottmeier Illustrations by Jesus Poom

Printed in Great Britain
by Amazon